"Crenshaw and Snapp offer us a story for the ages. It is a call to never settle for an ordinary life or a predictable God."

— DAN B. ALLENDER, PhD, president, Mars Hill Graduate School; author of *The Wounded Heart* and *To Be Told*

"Authentically powerful. Metaphorically creative. Poetically inspired. Spiritually profound. This is a book that will help readers understand a woman's healing journey from depression to illumination."

— VICTOR SIERPINA, MD, director of integrative medicine family practice residency, University of Texas Medical Branch

"Betty's life and message personally touched me in one of those "dark nights of the soul." Her honesty, transparency, and incredible wisdom provide the perfect vessel to bring healing to the brokenhearted and hope for the weary. An inspiring read!"

— MELODY CARLSON, author of *Finding Alice*, *Crystal Lies*, and the TRUECOLORS series

"Crenshaw and Snapp have deftly woven into a single narrative the life, the teaching, and the words of Betty Skinner. Readers will find courage, hope, and comfort for the journey."

— PHYLLIS TICKLE, compiler of *The Divine Hours*

"*The Hidden Life* will be invaluable to countless women and men, assuring them that they are not alone in their interior trials and that such dark passages not only are new but can prove with faith and patience to be gateways to wisdom."

— STEVEN PRESSFIELD, author of *The Legend of Bagger Vance* and *Gates of Fire*

"This is a moving story, not only of a particular woman but of the way in which the human soul can journey through brokenness to new birthings. It is our story. It is our hope."

— DR. J. PHILIP NEWELL, author of *Listening for the Heartbeat of God*

"Betty Skinner directs our eyes toward what is beautiful, pleasing, and perfect both around us and within us. Through her unique insights into life and the glorious things of God, she makes sense of suffering. In an age confused about priorities and questions of purpose, her wisdom has never been needed more."

— JIM TOWEY, faith-based leader; former legal counsel to Mother Teresa

THE
HIDDEN
LIFE

Revelations from a Holy Journey

Kitty Crenshaw and Catherine Snapp, PhD

NAVPRESS®

BRINGING TRUTH TO LIFE

OUR GUARANTEE TO YOU

We believe so strongly in the message of our books that we are making this quality guarantee to you. If for any reason you are disappointed with the content of this book, return the title page to us with your name and address and we will refund to you the list price of the book. To help us serve you better, please briefly describe why you were disappointed. Mail your refund request to: NavPress, P.O. Box 35002, Colorado Springs, CO 80935.

The Navigators is an international Christian organization. Our mission is to reach, disciple, and equip people to know Christ and to make Him known through successive generations. We envision multitudes of diverse people in the United States and every other nation who have a passionate love for Christ, live a lifestyle of sharing Christ's love, and multiply spiritual laborers among those without Christ.

NavPress is the publishing ministry of The Navigators. NavPress publications help believers learn biblical truth and apply what they learn to their lives and ministries. Our mission is to stimulate spiritual formation among our readers.

© 2006 by Katharine Kirk Crenshaw and Catherine Ann Snapp

NAVPRESS, BRINGING TRUTH TO LIFE, and the NAVPRESS logo are registered trademarks of NavPress. Absence of ® in connection with marks of NavPress or other parties does not indicate an absence of registration of those marks.

ISBN 1-57683-883-8

Cover design by The DesignWorks Group, Charles Brock
Cover background photo by Photos.com; photo of Betty provided by authors.
Creative Team: Terry Behimer, Darla Hightower, Pat Reinheimer, Arvid Wallen

Some of the anecdotal illustrations in this book are true to life and are included with the permission of the persons involved. Betty Walthour Skinner, the subject of this book, is not to be confused with Betty Lee Skinner, author of best-selling *Daws* and a long-time Navigator.

Unless otherwise identified, all Scripture quotations in this publication are taken from the HOLY BIBLE: NEW INTERNATIONAL VERSION® (NIV®). Copyright © 1973, 1978, 1984 by International Bible Society. Used by permission of Zondervan Publishing House. All rights reserved. Other versions used include: the *Revised Standard Version Bible* (RSV), copyright 1946, 1952, 1971, by the Division of Christian Education of the National Council of the Churches of Christ in the USA, used by permission, all rights reserved; and the *New American Standard Bible* (NASB), © The Lockman Foundation 1960, 1962, 1963, 1968, 1971, 1972, 1973, 1975, 1977, 1995.

Crenshaw, Kitty, 1949-
The hidden life : revelations from a holy journey / by Kitty Crenshaw and Catherine Snapp.-- 1st ed.
p. cm.
Includes bibliographical references.
ISBN 1-57683-883-8
1. Spirituality. 2. Christian life. I. Snapp, Catherine, 1963- II. Title.
BV4501.3.C74 2006
248.4--dc22
2005010073

Printed in the United States of America

2 3 4 5 6 / 10 09 08 07 06

FOR A FREE CATALOG OF NAVPRESS BOOKS & BIBLE STUDIES,
CALL 1-800-366-7788 (USA) OR 1-800-839-4769 (CANADA)

DEDICATION

CONTENTS

"I have given them the glory that you gave me, that they may be one as we are one: I in them and you in me. May they be brought to complete unity to let the world know that you sent me and have loved them even as you have loved me."
John 17:22-23

For you died, and your life is now hidden with Christ in God.
Colossians 3:3

INTRODUCTION

What is the hidden life, this inner life? And why—when promised such a precious gift—do we fail to perceive it, trust it, and live it?

— BETTY WALTHOUR SKINNER

Hidden deep in each of our souls is a true self—the person God created us to be. When we were knit in our mother's womb, we were given this gift of a true self, and with it the ability to live in a place of perfect unity with the Father and with each other. Yet, throughout our lives we have all been wounded. So out of our fear and guilt and shame, we unconsciously add layer upon layer of protective casing around our souls, moving us further and further from that place of perfect peace, keeping our true self hidden from others and obscured from ourselves. Jesus came to remind us of our sacred heritage and waits longingly for us to dare to trust enough to travel inward to His heart of Love, uncovering more and more of our true identity—our hidden life.

This life of hiddenness has been lived in all the fullness of its pain and joy by our friend and spiritual mentor, Betty Skinner. Her intense yearning for God ultimately led her from terrible suffering with clinical depression into the place of promised peace and rest that we all long for.

Ironically, God divinely dropped us—two raucous, talkative seekers—into the life of this peaceful, gray-haired lover of solitude and silence, using her quiet wisdom and gentle heart to draw us back to believing Jesus, not just believing our beliefs about Him. After years of a close spiritual friendship, we were convinced that her story needed to be told and that for reasons known only to Him, God had chosen us for this sacred task. So we got all of our taping equipment together and spent seemingly endless hours at her little condo recording her memories and wisdom. As sweet and profound as these times talking together always were, it was even sweeter to experience the depth of love and wordless Presence that so often emerged in our silence together.

Betty invariably greeted us at the door with the mandatory welcoming hug that we had to fold in half for because she is not even five feet tall. The first thing you notice about her is the winsome radiance of her smile. Its warmth disarms and always invites. Her steady brown eyes are tender and so full of love they seem to pull you into her soul, or maybe their safety just opens yours. She is almost eighty now, with pure-white, short-cropped hair and beautifully real wrinkles that testify to a life lived in all its fullness. She possesses a keen mind, able to recall with exact precision details of events that occurred years ago and to quote chapter and verse from books that have impacted her through her many years of study. You will most often find her simply dressed in khakis, a cotton turtleneck, cotton sweater, and black leather tennis shoes. She exudes warmth and contentment. The day we arrived on her doorstep to begin taping, she was wearing the white sweat suit and deerskin slippers that we teasingly call her "saint suit" because all of that white with her snowy white, monkish haircut makes her look for all the world like a tiny, cherubic saint.

Betty, being Betty, opened her life to us as readily as she has opened the doors of all of her various homes to many people over the years—widely, freely, and holding the hope that it might speak to the wounded hearts of others. What emerged was a beautiful story of hope and deep healing that was birthed out of her suffering, her faithful practice of spiritual disciplines, her solitude in the midst of creation, and her silence before the loving Creator of it all. She willingly shared the most private and painful details of her life, but she would always move beyond the facts to the truth and wisdom God had revealed to her through those circumstances. With Betty, everything always comes back to the spiritual journey. At the end of each chapter, we have included some of the many pearls of profound wisdom God taught her throughout her life. These illuminations are offered in Betty's own words as encouragement to all of us as we persevere on our own journeys to the heart of Love.

Also sprinkled throughout the book are her poems—or "little meditations" as she calls them. Whenever she reads one of them to us, she invariably tilts her head to one side and, with a quiet chuckle, tenderly says, "That's a sweet one, isn't it?" She wrote these meditations over a period of forty years. They begin in the stark simplicity of a heart crying out in agony and move to a depth and beauty that could only come from the profound awareness that her cry was heard. Their beauty and coherence are not at all what one would expect from a patient locked in a psychiatric hospital. The thread that ran through Betty's writings then, as now, was an enduring hope in God's loving presence in all things and an intense desire for her life to be poured out in love to others. By offering these meditations now, she entrusts us with her heart. In so belonging to one another, we are drawn into unity with God.

Necessity requires that we distinguish her spoken words with quotation marks but truly all of the words in this book are Betty's as we have understood them. Her story bears witness to the truth that God is a self-bestowing God who persistently presses in to meet, to change, and to fill us in our deepest need with His healing Love. It is our privilege—and now yours—to have been given the gift that came from her suffering and perseverance. It is a deep and abiding testimony to the existence of a Reality that we often do not see beyond our own, One that will transform the lives of those human souls who are free and open enough to receive it. The great mystery, though, is that so few of us seem to choose to truly grasp this hidden Truth. Betty puts the question to us like this:

"What is the hidden life, this inner life? And why—when promised such a precious gift—do we fail to perceive it, trust it, and live it? It is difficult for us to grasp the truth that Jesus came not to astonish us with the great power and high visibility of God but rather to show us the way of hiddenness, powerlessness, and humility. In contrast to our culture that applauds the upward mobility of man, the inner life affirms that God's path is the descending way. It leads us to a deeper understanding that, in His eyes, the most significant is often the most hidden.

"This contemplative life flows from a pure heart that has persevered through much suffering and found its way to the Source. When we finally come to see that our desire for God is an echo of God's far more encompassing and passionate desire for us, we can offer others a glimpse of light in the midst of their confusion, darkness, and pain. It is the love, hope, and encouragement of the One in Whom all is lost, yet all is found.

"Hopefully, in God's goodness and time, a tremendous paradox will be revealed to us—that what we now see as suffering and death is in Reality a hidden time of awakening and rebirth."

A circle full of ripples
from one pebble in a pond
fades unobtrusively
into forever
like a quiet life
poured out in love.

Our heart's desire is to offer you the gift of a spiritual friendship with Betty in the hope that her life's story might provide a path for your own healing into wholeness and make you a little more homesick for God. Our saintly friend walks more slowly now, but as we continue our journey together, she gently says to us all:

"Take His hand now, even as I am offering you mine, and in the warmth of such an all-compelling love, let us follow Him together."

Journeying together,

Kitty and *Cathy*

Lord,
My emptied heart is Yours.
Your living river runs
pure and sure
straight through it.
It washes all my pain away
and cleanses every wound.
I see You
in the gold of its reflections
before the dark appears.
I hear You
in the magic of its music,
in the song the rapids give.
I feel You
in the soft moss atop its rocks
that gathers up the morning dew
and holds each raindrop new.
Yet so much eludes and haunts me;
so much I long to know
lies hidden deep beneath
Your living river's flow.
In time I'll find the answers;
I know that they are there.
I'll find them alone with You, Lord,
quietly in prayer.

BWS

Chapter One

The

Invisible Foundation

All right Lord, I've been reading about what a good Christian woman should do and how she should live her life, but I want to say to You that it's not working for me. You promised me joy, You promised me peace, You promised me wholeness, and I'm not experiencing any of this. My life is a total disaster. There's got to be another way. I do not doubt Your promises, but I don't understand how to find them.

That was a long time ago—1968. The country had just awakened from "Happy Days" and found itself mired in a full-blown cultural revolution. The Beatles had landed to fuel the fire that Elvis started, the intensity of the Civil Rights Movement reverberated throughout the South, hippies were tripping in Haight-Ashbury, the Vietnam war was exploding, President Kennedy had been assassinated, and women were just beginning to flex their political muscles in the fight for equality. Unbeknownst to her, a similar revolution was brewing in the hidden life of Betty Walthour Skinner. She was forty-two years old, mother of four, wife of a very successful businessman and community leader, suburban socialite, Sunday school teacher, civic volunteer—and crippled by debilitating depression. Her perseverance on her long and arduous journey through pain has led her to the limitless peace and joy we all seek. The world is still in chaos, but Betty is well and whole and a powerful force for love. Now she shares that journey with us in the hope that, as she says, "many, many people might be blessed." This is how it began.

In 1926, Betty Walthour was born into the furnace of the Deep South. It was a time when oscillating fans held families together in the sultry days of summer. Children were obedient, fathers came home at 5:00, mothers wore aprons, and black maids shelled peas and cleaned the house for $2.50 a week. The Walthour house was one of the many grand and genteel antebellum houses in Birmingham, Alabama. Ceilings were high with fireplaces in every room, and there was a bedroom for every person—even the servants. Social standing was prescribed at birth and everyone knew his or her place. Betty's mother, Annie Tartt Walthour, was one of the many steel magnolias cast in that fire, and she had no doubt that her two beautiful daughters would also fit neatly into that mold. She was short and rather plump, but charming, fun, and always meticulously well-groomed and coiffed. She understood and thrived in the culture where all proper southern ladies wore pretty dresses, went to parties with a lovely, shy smile, and never, ever did any kind of work. That was what the black housekeeper or, more accurately in those days, the maid was for, and she did all of the cooking and cleaning.

Betty loved her little brothers and sister but didn't spend much time with them. She was, after all, the oldest, and Russell, who was closest to her in age, was always on the move with his friends, all of whom Annie Tartt hated. Charlie and Betty were closer because they were more alike. He was quiet and studious. He excelled at school because he had decided early on that he wanted a career in the military. Betty would sometimes wander into his room and they would talk for a while — it was just kid talk but it was talk and he was listening. Missie, the baby, was pretty — Annie Tartt's ideal little girl. She loved ballet and all things feminine and twirled endlessly around the living room in her pink satin toe shoes with the ribbons that wrapped miraculously up her lovely, muscled legs without drooping down as Betty's stockings did on Sundays when she got dressed for church.

To her mother's great consternation, Betty refused to fit into the role that was cast for her and proved to be much more like her father, Russell. He was a quiet, unpretentious, introverted military man who loved the serenity of his garden and the security of the military system. Betty, too, was an introvert and would much rather spend hours alone in her cozy attic room building intricate plastic airplane models than dress up to go to the parties her mother scheduled for her. Annie Tartt paid little attention to her exasperating eldest child except to yell from the bottom of the stairs, "Betty, get down here! It's time for your tap-dancing lessons!"

When Betty was ten years old, Russell moved his young family to Clemson, South Carolina, where he took a job at the university teaching military science. Betty loved to work with her father in the garden, planting seedbeds or jumping into the huge piles of colorful, crunchy autumn leaves they raked together. She kept her horse, Dixie, her billy goat, and her chickens in the backyard and delighted in running all sweaty and barefoot full blast through the cool, sand-bottom stream near their house.

"My father and I were very close because his quiet, easy manner wasn't threatening to me. He could be tough and very disciplined, but he was my father, teacher, friend, and mentor all wrapped up in the spit and polish of a military uniform. One summer, he and I sat together for hours on the divan picking out my first saddle for Dixie from the Sears and Roebuck catalog. It was a very special saddle to me because by giving it to me, my father was accepting and affirming me in who I was.

"On Sundays, we always went to the Presbyterian church together as a family. Daddy insisted on that. In true military fashion, we would dress up, line up, and march in — third pew from the front, left side, every Sunday. Mama didn't like it much and resented having to go. She much preferred her bridge and Junior League groups and was never interested in church activities of any kind. I loved the little gray stone church, though. It was all warm and cozy inside, and the graceful white steeple, with the little cross on top, seemed to me to be reaching all the way up to God. Enclosing the church grounds, the parsonage, and the old cemetery was a low wall made of the same gray stone and a narrow concrete sidewalk that was perfect for roller skating. The wall was made for resting, and the steeple — that pure white steeple — for me anyway, was made for gazing.

> *The gentleness of Christ*
> *its tender warmth of feeling*
> *its warmth of affection*
> *its love in all its depth and delicacy*
> *caresses and fills me*
> *like soft white clouds*
> *around a mountaintop.*

"My grandmother, Nannie, came with us to church when she was visiting from Birmingham. She was quiet and almost deaf, but she and I would sing our hearts out during the services, particularly at Christmas. She read mesmerizing stories about Jesus and different missionaries to me at night that gave me a deep sense that maybe one day I might be a medical missionary in a faraway country. They seemed to lead such exotic and wonderful lives. For as long as I can remember, I have felt the warm drawing power of God's love and wanted to serve Him in some way. I had a sense that God loved me just as I was."

When she was twelve, Betty was finally old enough to be confirmed in the church, and she was very excited and serious about the ceremony. Her mother dressed her up in a short, lavender smocked dress with a matching lavender, satin sash that tied with a big bow in the back. She proudly recited her vows with a strong, clear voice and all of her heart. At the end of the ceremony, Pastor Crouch gave her a sweet form letter that he gave to all the confirmands commending her on her commitment to Jesus. Betty was so proud of it that she took the money she had earned selling eggs from her chickens and rode her bike down the dirt road to the general store to buy a frame for the letter. It is still hanging on her bedroom wall sixty-seven years later.

> My Dear Betty,
>
> It was a fine thing you did when you stood before the pastor and promised to love and follow the Lord Jesus. My heart was full of joy and pride as you stood there and answered those serious questions. I pray that you may always live up to the vows you took. You are now a follower of the greatest King of all, our Lord Jesus, and if you are willing, He will use you every day in His service.
>
> Lovingly Yours,
> Ralph A. Crouch

When Betty turned fifteen, rumors of imminent war were clouding the horizon. Colonel Walthour was called to active duty, so he moved his family to Union, South Carolina, where he was put in command of an infantry division. He became so devoted to the men in his division that when the governor of Alabama offered him a promotion, he turned it down because it meant he would have to leave his men and sit behind a desk in Montgomery. Annie Tartt was beside herself when he declined the prestigious post because it would have meant a significant pay raise, a silver star on his uniform, and white-gloved dinner parties in the state capitol.

Russell and Annie Tartt lived in separate worlds. They were so different in every way, and neither seemed to be able to understand the other. They didn't know each other because they didn't know themselves; their hearts were hidden from each other. He was quietly slipping into a corner emotionally and shutting down, but she was so caught up in other things that she couldn't see that he was struggling with depression and that their older daughter carried his genes.

Illumination

For most of my life, I have been a seeker, searching and longing to live from a deeper place. On a rainy day many years ago, I stood silently and gazed at the mist that had crept in and covered the inside of my window so completely that I could barely see outside. As I contemplated the patterns the fog created, several tiny droplets came together and formed a single drop of condensation that slowly made its way down the pane of glass, clearing the mist from a narrow strip on the window and allowing me to see with clarity the astonishing beauty of my rain-refreshed backyard.

As I look back on my life's journey—and retrospect is such a beautiful view—I have learned that, just as the mist of our uncertainty coalesces and then opens us to glimpses of brilliant hope and vision, so, too, our times of darkness and pain reveal and illuminate the mystery and beauty of our true self hidden within. As you'll see, I have been through the dark and lonely places. I know the suffering and the pain of this inner journey, but I also have come to know the One who continues to lead me through it. As we choose to embrace the joys and the sorrows of each necessary season in faith and trust, the fog shrouding our soul slowly lifts and we behold, as in a glass, His glory and our glory in Him. Gradually then, we begin to mirror this eternal light of Love, claiming our true nature (see 2 Corinthians 3:18). After almost eighty years, I still can't explain it, but I can tell you that it is so because I have experienced it.

Jesus is not primarily a teacher of information or morals. His teachings go much deeper than that. He is a teacher of a way or a path that leads to change and transformation and a new heart brought about by a surrendered life deeply centered in God. Jesus challenges us to abandon the wide, easy path of conventional wisdom and embark on the long, difficult, and narrow path of divine wisdom that leads those of us who choose to follow away from temporal values centered in ourselves toward eternal values centered in God. He is always lovingly and compassionately inviting His followers to a different way of seeing and living.

Prayerfully, may my story and the illuminations that close each of these chapters be an encouragement and a light on the path for your journey home.

Betty

From the tears of my own confession
That flowed with the touch of His kiss
It was this
His caress, His compassion
That compelled me
To journey deep inside
Where all the beauty of forgiveness hides
Asleep and silent, still
Until aroused and summoned at His will.

At times it seemed I journeyed all alone.
'Twas I that lost my way.
For faith and trust eluded me
And fear engulfed me
In a darkness so profound
That all my senses rose then fell
And mocked me with their falsehoods.
Then died to temporal things
In silence, without a sound.

Yet, in this darkest midnight,
My only light, that of my heart's desire,
My every substance melted by its fire,
I recognized the Stranger, my Beloved,
My Companion through the years.
For sense and intellect were gone.
In His eternity of forgiveness,
My faith grew strong, my fears grew dim
And there was nothing, nothing, nothing.
　　Only Him.

BWS

CHAPTER TWO

GATHERING
MIST

Betty was seventeen when World War II changed everyone's world.
Russell's battalion was transferred to Colorado, so the Walthours had
to pick up and move again, leaving their home and lifestyle forever. Because
of the housing shortage brought on by the war, they were forced to live with
another family in a tiny house provided by the military and struggle for what
little private space there was. Of course, they couldn't take Dixie or the billy
goat and chickens Betty loved so much, so her world changed drastically
overnight. For the first time in her life, she tasted the bitter reality of change
and loss. She was put in a Catholic girl's school where she couldn't keep up
academically or socially, and her beloved friend and father was sent off to
war. The commander of a battalion on the European front had been killed,
and the army ordered Russell to take over immediately. He had to abruptly
leave his men and family to go directly into the last and bloodiest conflict
of World War II—the Battle of the Bulge. Sixty thousand troops were lost
that savage winter, and Colonel Walthour stood day after day watching
young men collapse into their deathbeds of bloody snow.

Annie Tartt moved the children back to the comforting familiarity of South Carolina when he was shipped overseas. In the summer that she was nineteen, Betty's father returned to them unexpectedly. The army called it battle fatigue and had sent him to one of the huge Miami Beach hotels that had been converted into military hospitals for R&R (rest and relaxation). In early June, they allowed him to come home for a family visit and Annie Tartt quickly saw that something was very wrong. Russell was acting strangely and incessantly paced around the dining-room table muttering softly and fretfully swinging his gold pocket watch. She became so worried about his bizarre behavior that she hid their old shotgun behind the cabinet in the garage and asked the army to send him back to the hospital early, which they did.

"One hot day in July, I was upstairs at my desk when I heard the doorbell ring. I opened the door and two army officers in dress uniforms asked to see my mother. I offered them a seat on the blue velvet settee in our parlor and went to the kitchen to find her. Mama came out and thanked the officers for coming but showed no reaction to the telegram that they handed her. It was the standard War Department one received by so many other families in those days. 'The War Department regrets to inform you . . .'"

"After the men left, Mama just sat on the couch, so I went back upstairs to my room feeling a strange, vague numbness. Mama didn't tell me what was in the telegram but somehow I knew that Daddy was dead. It would be years later before I found out that he had hanged himself with his belt from a rafter in his hospital room. The raw truth of his suicide was never discussed. Suicide was just not something you discussed in polite company."

The army report said that Russell had had a nervous breakdown two years earlier, while serving on the front line. He had gone up to check on his men, being very careful to leave his Jeep and driver in what he thought was a safe place, but when he returned he found only the smoldering remains of his car and his young driver blown apart by an artillery shell. It proved to be more than Russell could bear.

"I wasn't prepared for my father's death. My world as a child had been far removed from the brutalities of reality. Pain struck deeply for the first time and I didn't know what to do with it. We had been taught to 'keep a stiff upper lip.' Feelings and emotions were suppressed, never expressed. Yet on that pain-filled day in July, for the very first time, a vague intuitive sense of reality awakened within me. It shadowed me like a mist on a gray day. I couldn't see through it, but I knew it was there—and it never left me.

"Daddy's funeral at Arlington National Cemetery was impressive and befitting his rank. Beautiful horses pulled the caisson bearing his flag-draped casket. There was an honor guard and the twenty-one-gun salute followed by a bugler playing taps. Mama was quiet; I remember that she didn't cry or hug me, and we never spoke of Daddy again."

The war had taken her husband, her home, and her lifestyle, so Annie Tartt was forced to move with her four children back to Alabama to share her grandparents' house with her widowed sister's family. She arrived wearing her mink coat and diamond wristwatch with her Junior League membership intact, never breaking her social stride. Her four children and Virgie, their faithful housekeeper, followed her.

Betty went off to the University of Alabama, and Annie Tartt took a job in Miss Janie's dress shop in Birmingham. She hated having to work but she needed the money, and at least at Miss Janie's she could be around beautiful clothes. She continued to try to teach Betty the value of society parties and lovely dresses but Betty just would not learn. She felt like a caged bird in those clothes, in that world. Her mother would send boxes and boxes of dresses from Miss Janie's to Betty at the Kappa Delta house, but she only wore them because women weren't allowed to wear pants to school in those days. As soon as classes were over, she put her comfortable pants back on. The more her mother persisted, the more Betty resisted.

"I didn't know why I couldn't fit the mold that my mother had chosen for me. I just knew that it didn't feel good to be forced into it. I didn't understand yet that Mama was innocent in this, that she pressured me out of her own fear and unhealed childhood pain. It would take many more years before I began to understand that we wound others out of our own wounding. My mother and I stayed in conflict and along with the conflict came a deep sense of shame, guilt, and fear because I couldn't live up to her expectations. I felt enormous anger, but being an introvert, I suppressed it. This created a tremendous amount of inner turmoil that slowly began to eat away at me, eroding my self-esteem and my sense of self."

I long to be loved as I am.
out from the mold
of what others would have me be
free of demand, of stress
to be known as I am
yet loved.
What a creative thing this would be.

In the winter of 1947, Betty was to be presented at the Redstone Ball at the Birmingham Country Club. Annie Tartt was beside herself with excitement and dragged her daughter to yet another fitting with Miss Ayers, the dressmaker for all of Birmingham's finest ladies. Betty was furious. She didn't want to go but was also fighting the guilt she felt about her feelings toward her mother, so she sat in the front seat of the car in complete silence, rigid with rage, not moving a muscle, physically and emotionally withdrawing into her pain. Very gradually, this hidden, unconscious way of coping with fear and anger, which she adopted as a girl dealing with her mother, became the pattern for dealing with conflict that she carried into her adult years. Eventually, it would insidiously, yet mercifully, lead to her breakdown.

When she was twenty, Betty was invited to Jacksonville, Florida, for her friend Dottie's debutante party. She had known Dottie since childhood because their families had been neighbors and close friends during the Depression. Bryant, Dottie's brother, didn't pay much attention to Betty until the night before she was supposed to leave, but after dinner at his family's house, he asked her to go out on the screen porch and talk. They sat on the swing and he asked her if she would stay a little longer so they could go on a date the next night. She ended up staying so long that Dottie finally had to ask Betty to go home. She was bowled over by romantic love, and on June 12, 1948, Betty and Bryant were married in a beautiful church ceremony. Her handsome brothers, Russell and Charlie, proudly walked her down the aisle in their highly starched, gold-braided and buttoned military dress whites. Russell was a graduate of West Point, and Charlie from Virginia Military Institute.

Bryant took his pretty young bride back to Jacksonville to begin their family. She was quite immature and their backgrounds were very different. He was from a powerful, rough and tumble, mostly male family in Florida that placed a high premium on work and productivity, and she had been raised in the southern culture of those days in which women were not supposed to be anything other than pretty. Because of that, Betty had no concept of what it meant to do work of any kind. The early years of their marriage were good, but when the newness wore off and ordinary life set in with its schedules and demands, their radical personality differences caused their relationship to splinter. Betty had married a man whose voice was as powerful as her mother's.

Bryant and his mother-in-law were both so strong that they butted heads at first but soon became fast friends. Annie Tartt would get lonely and call Bryant to take her dancing at the George Washington Hotel. Betty never wanted to go with them because their energy was too much for her, so Bryant and Annie Tartt would go downtown together and drink and dance all night long.

Bryant loved parties and frenzied activity of any kind: ball games, fishing trips, or gambling junkets. And he was always building things: not just houses but whole communities. He quickly became an extremely successful businessman whose bottom line was, "What did you get done today?" Betty had a very different agenda. She was as compulsive about her need for privacy as he was about his need for people and productivity. She loved solitude and quiet, gray days and sunsets, and simple things like walking on the beach and listening to the soothing rhythm of the waves. She had a sense of the possibility that there could be a rhythm and a balance to life, because she saw it in nature and longed for it in her own world. She had no language for these contemplative yearnings at that time, just a gentle tug in her heart to "be" rather than "do."

Their first child, Bryant Jr., was born in 1949 when Betty was twenty-three, just before their first anniversary. Three more babies came along, one right after the other. Charlie followed Bryant Jr., then Betsy and Russell. In those days, having that many children wasn't unusual, and being so young and immature, Betty had absolutely no idea of the amount of work and stress involved in caring for them. Bryant, like most men of that day, was no help at all.

As was her pattern, she just blindly did what Bryant, her mother, the culture, and everyone around her expected. She was living out her life frantically and unconsciously, trying to satisfy voices that told her she wasn't good enough, smart enough, productive enough, pretty enough, thin enough, spiritual enough, and on and on. Those voices were so loud and so pervasive that they drowned out the still, small voice of the Divine within that was trying to get her attention. Guilt, confusion, and shame gradually covered her true self with layer after layer of false behaviors she used to protect herself, and the gift of a precious soul, uniquely created by God, was lost to itself and to the world.

Illumination

Suffering has so much to teach us. It is not a punishment but the divine route to resting in God. It is a call to faith, a test of character, a means of loving discipline, an encouragement to prayer. If we can see our suffering as sharing, in a small way, in Christ's passion — His willingness to surrender in trust to that which was done to Him — we, too, will be graced with the strength to embrace it and learn from it. By embracing our suffering and allowing it to do its work of breaking through the protective walls we have constructed around our hearts, we become more vulnerable and honest. This moves us to a deeper understanding of our shared brokenness, opening us to a compassionate dimension within our hearts, allowing us to slowly change our focus from ourselves to the needs and the hurts of others. It awakens us to the truth of our lives, and we begin to see reality as it is rather than the way we think it should be or wish it was. Once we choose to see this with the eyes of trust, we are no longer living in illusion, and God can graciously begin to heal us.

Painful circumstances and relationships that seem so defeating and discouraging are most often sacred gifts holding the seeds of our healing if we will embrace them, persevere through them, and allow them to change us and wake us up to a whole new way of seeing. So often when we are hurting, we run from one thing to the next, frantically looking for a quick fix that will ease our searing pain and restore things to the way they used to be. However, God is not seeking restoration but transformation. The more we submit to and participate in the mystery of this purifying work, the more we begin to experience a sense that everything, even our darkest pain, is held in divine love.

Our Lord reaches out from the Cross to embrace us with both arms. One is the arm of sorrow, suffering, and pain, and the other is the arm of peace, love, and joy. We cannot have one without the other. As we welcome our pain and unmet longings with hope, we open to the divine embrace. We are, at last, resting in God. This is the hope that Paul knew when he exhorted us to rejoice and give thanks in all things (see 1 Thessalonians 5:16-18).

I need say no more just now, dear friend, for such a love that knows another's pain is their nourishment, hope, and encouragement, and this I long to be through our dear Lord, who turned my pain to love for you.

Betty

Oh, Good Jesus,
    Hear me, hold me, love me
       in this, the season of
          my spirit's loss and grieving,
       in the anguish of my waiting,
       in the silence of familiar voices gone,
       in the pain of all the change,
       in the twilight of my years
          before perfection dawns
          and I am gone.

Oh, Good Jesus,
    I try the letting go,
       to understand my weakness,
       to trust You in my darkness,
       to make room for Your grace to heal.
    Yet there is no return,
       only the echo of my own crying.
    It seems I, too, with You,
       am caught between the nails.

Oh, Good Jesus,
    In this holy place of crucifixion,
       broaden the boundaries of my heart.
       Soften the places that
          defend, define and deny.
       Teach my heart to love.
       Make it a refuge for others
       who, too, are caught
          between the nails.

BWS

CHAPTER THREE

SECRET

FEAR

In 1950, Betty's younger brother, Charlie, was sent away to fight in the Korean War. They were very close because they were both reserved and quiet and had always been able to understand each other. Betty was proud of him. He was tall and handsome and gentle like her father—a natural leader, graduating at the top of his class at Virginia Military Institute. She felt safe with him, like a sister feels with a brother who has shared a lifetime of quiet heart connection, living through so much of the same pain, change, and loss together. The summer before he left, they had had a sweet time together playing with her baby and talking about his new girlfriend, his military ambition, and his dreams for the future. Now she missed him terribly. Oddly, she really wasn't concerned much for his safety because she was so naïve. It never occurred to her that young men might die again so soon after the Great War. After all, Korea was such a small war in such a small country so far away.

She was thrilled to find a letter from him in the mailbox, but her heart sank as her eyes skimmed quickly across the pages. Charlie sounded terribly depressed as he wrote about the horrors of war and the "God forsaken" place he was in. He asked her to promise him three things if anything happened to him: First, she was not to let them leave his body in Korea; second, she was to use his $5,000 government insurance policy to educate her children; and third, she was to make sure that any other money of his went to Virgie, their old housekeeper. It sounded like a premonition of death, which frightened her and triggered a pain so deep she wasn't able to hold it. She carefully put the letter in the desk drawer beside her bed, repressed the flood of surfacing emotion, and put the fear out of her mind.

Three months later she got the phone call from her mother that at some unconscious level she had been waiting for. Annie Tartt very calmly told Betty that she had some bad news. She had received another telegram from the War Department informing her that Charlie had been killed in action. A single bullet had penetrated the zipper of his flak jacket and exploded in his chest. The ponderous silence that surrounded her father's suicide had weighed so heavily on Betty's memory and feelings that she repressed all emotion when the news of Charlie's death came. All she knew to do was what she had learned from her mother, so she stuffed the overwhelming pain deep into her soul and went on with her busy life. As with her father, her brother was never spoken of again. She never dealt with his loss, never cried a tear. She just didn't think about it.

She had been hiding her feelings from herself for so long that she couldn't find them for her children. With each of her succeeding pregnancies, Betty suffered severe postpartum depression that lasted as long as six months and manifested in an extreme detachment from her babies. She took care of their physical needs but struggled to nurture them emotionally. She never rocked or held them any longer than was necessary and their crying made her frighteningly angry at times. As her postpartum eased, though, she became very involved in birthday parties, baby books, Cub Scouts, vacation Bible school, and all the normal motherly activities.

Betty was a lot of fun, physically active, and engaged with the children. She spent an enormous amount of energy trying to do what "good mothers" did, but she was unable to feel what "good mothers" felt. On the surface, though, her world was safe, secure, and predictable.

"I remember a lot of days when the kids were such cute ages and we had a lot of fun together. I always liked to garden. I was planting some geraniums along the hedge and was so intent on getting them in the ground, I wasn't paying attention to what the kids were doing. All of a sudden it was suppertime and I needed to run to the store to pick up something for us to eat. I had a little blue Plymouth coupe that my father-in-law had given me that the kids called the "Blue Beetle." We all piled into the Beetle and took off, but halfway to the store this horn started tooting in back of me and a man kept pointing at the back of my car. Finally, he came up beside me and yelled, 'Lady, do you realize that you've got red geraniums lined up all along the bumper of your car?!' The kids had taken them out as fast as I was putting them in the ground and had put them on the rear bumper. Yeah, I did . . . I had some fun times like that with the children."

> There are a thousand things
> I must do, Lord.
> You know this.
> Clothes to be mended,
> pictures to be hung,
> towels to be returned,
> parties to be given,
> people to be loved.
> Yet I cannot seem to free myself from You.
> You keep pulling at my heart.
> When I can be torn no longer
> I stop

surrender all of me to You.
And in this moment there is
such joy, such peace, such fullness.
Why didn't I stop sooner, Lord,
Heed the calling of my heart?
For I easily could have missed You
in the thousand things I still must do.

Betty's fear of the unknown and the unplanned created so much inner turbulence for her that she tried to avoid them at all costs. She found what little peace she could by meticulously planning her day around the children's school activities, her community activities, and all of the million things a mother has to do to manage an active home. Living with Bryant, though, made this impossible. With hurricane force, he would blow in the door and decimate her most carefully laid plans igniting a fury inside of her she had no way of releasing. Desperate for security and survival, she tried to create a tiny bubble to live in and was totally unaware that fear of losing control was fueling every moment of her life. This way of coping caused her to expend enormous energy propping up and maintaining the illusion that she could make her world predictable and secure.

Her little world exploded in 1964 when Bryant came in and announced that he was selling the house and was going to build a massive housing development on 500 acres of woodland in what was then considered the boondocks of Jacksonville. He rallied the children to the cause as Betty watched in disbelief. Bryant was such a great salesman that he worked the kids into a frenzy of excitement with outrageous tales of backwoods adventure. They were thrilled with the prospect of this Huck Finn-like existence. To Betty, nothing could have been more threatening, but within the month, her safe, suburban, predictable world was obliterated. They packed up and moved into the woods — miles away from friends, stores, schools, or conveniences.

Suddenly, her life became one over which she had very little control and absolutely no authority. For Bryant, everything was on the line, so he came home at night ferociously tense, ratcheting up the pressure on everyone. He quickly built a house and began to entertain there frequently and spontaneously in an effort to sell people on the idea of living in his development. He constantly committed them to parties, civic functions, and social activities without checking with Betty, decimating the order and structure she tried so desperately to hang on to in her fearful little world. The pressure in the house was palpable.

Life was not all bad, though. There were wonderful advantages to living in the woods. Betty was very outdoorsy and loved to hunt and fish with the boys or watch Bryant Jr. and Betsy ride their horses. She played tennis and worked in her garden and enjoyed it very much, but always she yearned for more time to herself. The demands of her husband, his business, and four children, though, didn't allow for that.

Occasionally, she would sneak away to walk on the beach, but that would upset Bryant because, as he saw it, she hadn't adequately accomplished the tasks he had outlined for her on the many lists, instructions, and memos he left for her. If she spent all day raking the yard, he would come home and find the only leaf she missed. It seemed she never got to the bottom of her task list in a day and the next day always held another one. She hated the expectations he put on her and became increasingly resentful but was much too fearful to speak up; the price of confronting him was too high. Each day brought more stress, more bills, more demands, and far too little security. Betty loved her children as best she could, but she was unable to meet their emotional needs and had no idea of what it meant to "be" with them in any deep sense. She was unconsciously detached from their hearts because she was so detached from her own. Ultimately, it caused fractures in their relationships that would take many years to heal. She became more and more guilt-ridden and unable to cope, feeling that she wasn't a good wife or mother and knowing that she wasn't meeting any of her family's needs. All of this guilt obscured her sense of worth, causing her to flounder in a sea of negative self-talk. Outside the reach of her awareness, fear and anger were slowly gnawing away at her energy and sense of self, crippling her more deeply, day after day. Depression was creeping in very gradually, insidiously and relentlessly, because she was separated from her true self, compulsively operating from other people's voices and expectations.

> *Who am I anyway?*
> *Others see absolutely nothing.*
> *They crucify with their tongues.*
> *They force me into a vacuum.*
> *I am lonely.*
> *I am empty.*
> *I am nothing.*

"As much as I wanted to keep up with Bryant, I couldn't. As I saw it, he was dynamic and growing and I was still stuck in my little box with my heels dug in, so the guilt feelings began to increase, which led to a deep sense of unworthiness. He was always talking and moving so fast, making plans and changing them as soon as he made them, and keeping things all stirred up. He and his way of life were very threatening to me. I never told him I didn't want to do the things he was always demanding of me; it wasn't worth the risk. I just emotionally shut him out and hoped the things he was throwing at me wouldn't happen. I was in tremendous conflict internally yet very compliant externally. This split, which fostered such disharmony in my life, eventually triggered my depression. I had allowed Bryant's voice rather than God's to become the controlling factor in my life. I was not growing as a person, and I was not becoming the person God had created me to be. I wasn't becoming anything and it was destroying everything."

Just like her mother, Bryant was forcing his agenda on her. Just like her mother, he was pushing her into a mold she didn't fit, and she didn't feel loved for who she was. Once again, she found herself unable to please the most important person in her world. The pain of this rejection was immense, but she repressed it, bearing it in silence. The downward depressive spiral deepened. Like a sea anemone when touched, she reflexively drew back into herself for protection and survival.

Illumination

As we live more and more from the deeper dimensions of the hidden life, we very slowly begin to realize that we have allowed our illusions to separate our hearts from God, others, and ourselves. We have been conditioned to think that we do not have enough. We need more—be it attention, affection, esteem, control, or security—so we live with constant anxiety that drives us to control, compete, and compare ourselves to others. This process leaves us experiencing a great deal of shame, further alienating us from what is real and from who we are. It takes courage, trust, and faith beyond all doubt to detach from these insatiable fears and needs that enslave us and keep us from peace. As long as we remain fearful, we will remain isolated and limited in our capacity to relate to others in a compassionate way. We will continue to live in illusion rather than authentic love.

Illusions are the product of the false-self system. It is our way of seeing and hearing that has been formed by the wounds of our cultural conditioning, our attachments, and our false gods. It is how we see things before we truly see, how we hear things before we truly hear, and how we live out of balance without knowing we are out of balance. Illusions separate us from the heart of God, keeping us imprisoned in our fears and self defenses, bound by our opinions and judgments, always in denial and always reflecting on self. As long as we live in illusion, we cannot see things as they really are and we cannot see God, who is Ultimate Reality.

We don't tend to see our illusions but other people do. These illusions and excessive behavior patterns take us down in a desperate struggle with despair and pain. The truth, though, is that the struggle can be a wonderful gift because if we will submit to it, God will take us down to that ground on which we can finally stand. When we hit the bottom, we wake up and begin to sense a need for change — that what we have been doing isn't working. This waking up happens as we faithfully come to prayer asking for the desire and the grace to see. In His time, God lovingly and gently touches our heart, allowing us to identify the false ways we have looked for security, control, affection, and esteem, and begin to see things as they are, not as our false self tells us they are.

Once we are awake, there is work to do and changes to make, but if we refuse to make them we are not going to grow. We are going to stay stuck rather than break through to hearing the transforming inner voice of Love, seeing with new eyes, and loving with a new heart. As we drop our illusions and move into love, things don't affect us personally anymore, so we don't have to defend ourselves, define other people, or deny our reality anymore. Now we are free and our lives slowly begin to come into balance.

Prayerfully, may the Spirit of Love work within us a transformation that will open our eyes and move us to that great, free plateau of love.

Betty

Jesus.......weeping over Jerusalem.
Jesus.......waiting at the tomb of Lazarus.
Jesus.......in the garden sweating blood.
Jesus.......revealing the heart of God.

Jesus, in my solitude,
*   show me Your face*
*   stained with sweat,*
*   smeared with blood.*

Jesus, in my solitude,
*   through my tears,*
*   speak to me*
*   of Your pain,*
*   of Your passion.*

Jesus, remember me
*   when You come*
*   into Your kingdom.*

BWS

CHAPTER FOUR

ENVELOPING

DARKNESS

B etty's pattern of protecting herself from pain affected the whole family. The only way she knew how to deal with her suffering was to go back to her childhood pattern of detaching from it and, consequently, detaching from the responsibilities of her life and all of her family relationships. She spent hours and hours lost in one Christian book after another and took on more and more Christian activities outside of the house. She was in charge of activities at the Salvation Army, a summer camp at the YWCA, teaching Vacation Bible School and the Young Adults Sunday school at the Baptist Church, and teaching a teenager's Bible study for Young Life. Meanwhile, her children were hungry, and her husband was furious. This unconscious pattern of escape was especially subtle because she was doing the "Lord's work," but it was only deepening her despair and brokenness.

She was in her midthirties now and struggling to keep her head above water. Then she found an unlikely friend who gave her a little hope that things could be different. Popular author, Anne Morrow Lindbergh became a mentor of sorts to her through her best-selling book, *A Gift from the Sea*.

It touched a deep chord with many women by giving voice to their feelings in a time when men were in charge of all of the cultural, family, business, political, and religious systems. Lindbergh, married to a strong, famous, highly ambitious man, urged women to develop and live from their own unique center rather than being constantly drawn into and drained by the energy of their husbands. She encouraged women to take time to care for themselves, to simplify their external lives, and spend some time each day being still, quiet, and inwardly attentive to their own feelings and longings, and God's presence with them. She spoke of a solitude that could be therapeutic and life-giving rather than fearsome and debilitating. Betty was amazed to read that Lindbergh had the courage to leave her family and take a weeklong retreat just to be alone and walk on the beach. She described the feeling of being soothed by the rhythm of the waves and the freedom of quietly contemplating all that God was teaching her through the sights, smells, and sounds of the sea. These words deeply resonated with Betty and were awakening something within her while affirming her love for the sea and all of God's creation. On one of her own beach walks, she found a moon shell like one Anne Morrow used in her book to illustrate the need for focus and singleness of heart in the search for Truth. In the midst of the chaos in the world of her reality, Betty would gaze at that moon shell sitting on her desk and be reminded of her own need for singleness of purpose and total commitment to persevere into the heart of Love.

At times I struggle with what seems to be heavy chains!
They bind me.
For too often I lose sight of love.
I know it is God that is calling me at these times
to take another step into Love's bondage.
Yet as I follow Him as best I can,
in full commitment, I find the struggle ends.
The chains are lifted.

"In an odd way, Lindbergh's ideas made me more insecure because here was something I longed for desperately but didn't think I could ever attain. Claim a week to myself? I needed it desperately but was far too fearful to do it. Finally, I got up the courage to tell Bryant I wanted to rent a small place at the beach for a week. He said it was fine on the condition that I took all the kids, so I did. It was a disaster. I was sitting there with my nose in a book, totally disconnected from my four children, who were crying because they were having no fun at all crammed in this little house with no one to play with and nothing to do. They needed me to be crabbing and swimming and building sand castles with them, but I was totally detached, sitting there in my chair thinking about God, with my head in the clouds, reading Anne Morrow Lindbergh and Florence Nightingale!"

Her life at home continued to be chaotic, and on top of everything else she had to deal with, Betty had taken in her sister, Missie's, handicapped son, Pidge. Even in her dysfunctional state, she was still trying to be the perfect Christian woman. Pidge lived with them in the new house for almost two years, adding that much more pressure to an already incredibly tense situation. Betty kept the beds made and food on the table but her hold on reality and her emotional availability to her family had almost evaporated. What her family really needed she wasn't able to give them until much later in life — her loving presence and attention.

That was when Bryant — again — chose to sell their house. Even though that house had never felt like home to her, it was another huge blow to her sense of significance and security. Bryant's sister Dottie and her husband had finally agreed to move to Deerwood, Bryant's development in the woods, but they didn't want to build, so Bryant just sold them his own family's house. He came home one day and announced that they would have to build another house because Dottie had a deadline to be out of hers.

Loneliness
Is like a gray day by the sea.
Mist covers everything.
No thoughts, no feelings,
one sound, the ocean's voice,
and it says nothing.

During this tremendously dark time in 1966, Betty was miraculously given another ever-so-thin thread of hope to hold onto. As broken and fragmented as she was, she was still trying to keep up with five children who were entering their teens, take care of a busy, demanding husband, teach Sunday school, lead a Bible study for other people's teenagers, and minister to unwed mothers at the Salvation Army. Being so overcommitted, she was, of course, unprepared for the Bible study she had to lead the next day. She needed something to teach from, so she jumped in the Blue Beetle, ran down to Effie Sutton's bookstore, grabbed Emerson's *Essay on Friendship*, jumped back in the car, threw the bag on the backseat, and raced home to meet the kids and get supper ready before Bryant came barreling through the door.

"That night, I got in bed completely exhausted but I opened the book anyway, because I had to come up with some kind of a lesson for the next day. When I opened it, I was stunned. Bryant was reading a magazine right next to me, with no idea that lightning had just struck. Inside the jacket and the hardback cover of this book by Emerson was a different book entirely. The publisher had printed Henry Drummond's famous book on love, *The Greatest Thing in the World*, with the Emerson cover. I had bought a book on friendship but was holding a book about love. As I read it transfixed, I realized for the first time in my life that I didn't know one thing about how to love. I had been on the verge of quitting my volunteer teaching job at the Salvation Army because I couldn't get these unwed mothers to respond to me in the slightest. I suddenly realized that I was just teaching them; I wasn't loving them at all. All of this time I had been preaching to them, all dressed up in my big white Christian god-coat, with the attitude that they were just poor sinners I was there to save. This huge revelation came to me through that little book and not only changed the entire focus of my teaching—it changed the focus of my life. The next day I went back to the bookstore to see if all of the copies had been misprinted but mine was the only one. Imagine that.

"Drummond helped me see all of this by taking each one of love's characteristics listed in 1 Corinthians 13 and breaking them down one at a time. It seemed to me that God was saying very simply that learning to love was the only thing that mattered in life. It deeply spoke to me, and without saying a word to anyone, I took each virtue and very consciously practiced it for three months. I was still very scattered, my priorities were still very misplaced, I still knew absolutely nothing about myself, I still didn't understand that I needed to let go of all my striving and just be still and listen for God, but I was responding as best I could to what I felt was God's call. My desire to know Him was strong, and that desire eventually brought me to a deeper place. Many years later, He would use all of my brokenness and all I had learned from Drummond to offer a thread of hope to others who were struggling through the darkness. If we will persevere, nothing on our spiritual journey is wasted—it is all preparation."

Love is never merely following suit.
Love is always taking the initiative.
Love reaches out, but love accepts.
For love is seeing as God would see.
Love provides the spark, it turns the switch.
Love cleans, deepens, fills, breathes new air
frees another life
to know God's heart
to find love there.

Another book that impacted Betty was Oswald Chambers' *My Utmost for His Highest*. A friend had given it to her for Christmas, and she sat in the bay window of their house turning the little book over and over, just looking at it and feeling the soft leather. The gift touched her deeply, because it was the first time anyone had ever given her a religious book, and it was the first time anyone had affirmed her for who she was since her father gave her that saddle so many years ago. She read it without understanding much but always gleaned a little bit and it became her daily spiritual nurture. Chambers' words kept bringing her back to believing Jesus rather than just believing her beliefs about Him. Chambers was telling her that the way to life was through Jesus, and as she so sweetly says, "I was just foolish enough to believe it."

Even with the knowledge she was gaining, she was still far too busy and fragmented and not at all aware of her inner self. She still had no idea who Betty Skinner was, why she responded the way she did to people, why she experienced so much fear and anxiety, and why she wasn't able to meet the emotional needs of those in her world. She hadn't yet learned that beneath her false fears and protective behaviors was her true self—a place of peace and wholeness quietly calling her, yearning to get her attention. Paradoxically, she was using her spiritual books and activities as an escape, and these good things were actually separating her from her family and from the heart of God.

> *Are prayer and meditation*
> *a means of escape from reality?*
> *Or is it a time for gathering*
> *strength to face reality?*

The pressure Betty felt from Bryant was becoming so intense that she began to imagine that the things he was asking her to do were a lot more demanding than they really were. By the time a party or an event he had planned actually happened, she was so burned out from all of the energy she expended in negative anticipation that it was just hell for her. She would drag herself through it, gripped with fear, often spending most of the party hiding in the ladies' room. Her God-given natural tendency to solitude, warped by fear, became more and more obsessive. She began to fiercely protect her time alone. When Bryant announced another one of his plans for her, she had neither the strength nor the self-confidence to say no, so instead, she would tell herself and him that she didn't feel good and needed to stay home to rest. She began to actually believe this illusion.

"Once we were going with one of his friends on a big sailboat. I got seasick easily, so I was very anxious about the trip. I had so little self-respect that I didn't have the courage to say a simple little thing like, 'I'm sorry I can't go because I get too seasick.' All night I lay awake worrying because I was so afraid. I had totally lost the ability to speak for myself. As it turned out, the trip never even came off because the weather was terrible.

"I yearned to escape this frightening reality I was living in, so more and more I did it by staying inside—inside my house, inside my fear, inside my pain. Contrary to what I told myself, though, there was nothing in that kind of solitude that was helping me to get well or grow as a person. I was always anxious and worried, and fear was consuming me. I needed to get out and be with people, but I didn't know that then, I had to learn it. I stayed home but those were long, lonely, fragmented days."

I need encouragement, I need hope
I need to hang on to something
because I am sinking.
The accusations, the rebukes, the insults
How heavy the burden.
Oh, how lonely the heart.
And oh, how I yearn so often to be free.

Betty clung to the hope that she could be free and whole, but she was afraid—afraid she would spend the rest of her life mired in the painful chaos she was living. She was a prisoner in her own flesh. She knew there had to be more to life, and she was desperate to find it. The miracle was that she never lost the will to hope. She understood, on some deep, barely conscious level, that if she would persevere and be patient with the pace of grace, God would finally show her the way to peace. She couldn't communicate to anyone the depths of her pain, but she always had a sense that God understood. At some point, having no one in her life she could share these things with, she began putting all that she was feeling and experiencing on paper and shared it with Him.

"I don't know exactly why or even when this idea came to me that I should keep a ledger of deep-felt thoughts. I am convinced that in matters of the heart we are all alone, isolated, unable to communicate with others, even those we love very dearly. Our tears, our gifts, our hurts, our heartaches, our depressions, our decisions, our uncertainties, our good, and yes, our evil thoughts are all incommunicable. We cannot speak them or write them down. Yet I know that God has placed within me a hunger, a longing to communicate, to share, to give, to serve, to love. In desperation I turned to Him, for He seemed to understand and listen. So it was that I began to build a 'life hid with Christ in God.' This then might well be called 'My Hidden Life.'"

How do I build this "hidden life"?
By bringing to God each day,
My tears, my troubles, my defeats and my ruins.
And while I groan God builds,
Patiently, secretly, silently deep within me
The invisible, the unshakable foundations.

The children, now teenagers, deeply resented having a mother who was emotionally unavailable to them, so they dealt with their loss and anger as best they could and went about their lives without her. They were slipping away, and her marriage was deteriorating because she wasn't there for any of them. Gone was the mother who hunted and fished with her sons, who rode horseback with her daughter, who played tennis with Bryant. Gone was the smile and easy laugh that had warmed their home a long, long time before. She was drowning in self-pity, emotionally spent and terrified about what was happening to her. Fear was paralyzing her and her depression was mounting. Her family knew that something was very wrong, but they didn't see her pain, they only saw a very dysfunctional human being.

Suffering, suffering, suffering
Physical, mental, spiritual.
The pain is so great, unbearable
I surely will break.
Yet, Christ has promised
to make me whole.

Illumination

At some point in our lives, we all wrestle with failure. The sources may vary: broken relationships, financial difficulties, shattered dreams, spiritual drought, and darkness. Whatever the source, failure and the feelings that go with it touch us at our very core. Failure is a dark experience that tells us, even as we struggle to shut it out, that at some basic level of our being, we are inadequate, that somewhere in our lives we have not lived up to our own expectations or the expectations of others. These shame-filled feelings become a tear in the fabric of our personhood and our self-worth.

As believers, we need to be reminded that the Resurrection

threw out all the world's standards, expectations, and measurements. God does not look on our performance but rather on the desire of our hearts. Our success-oriented culture is much more interested in the bottom line than in the failed attempts along the way. In God's economy, neither failure nor success is good or bad. We have only to look into the lives of those in Scripture to see how God redeemed and honored the failed attempts of His children. Moses failed to enter the Promised Land, yet God saved a nation through him. David had an affair, murdered his friend, and failed to build the temple, yet God birthed the Savior through his lineage. The woman at the well was an adulteress who failed in her marriages, yet Jesus offered her life. The truth we learn from Jesus is that failure is not our ultimate enemy any more than success is our ultimate goal. His focus is never on our failure or our success but always on our potential for love, for truth, for trust, and for wholeness. Thus we never need to be discouraged but remain faithful.

Being faithful in failure does not mean to ignore, repress, or deny it or our feelings about it. Being faithful in failure means to see our failures, embrace them, and grow from them. Embracing our failure opens us up to what is real, to see things as they truly are, as painful as that may be. When we begin to accept our reality in this way, we can finally open to receive God's love, see ourselves as He sees us, be touched by His healing compassion and learn to offer it to others.

May the words on this page encourage us toward a new thought, the thought that amid all of our failed hopes, dreams, expectations, and opportunities, we belong to a God whose great love has transformed and changed forever the meaning of success and failure.

Resting in Hope,

Betty

Liberate me. Free me.
Lift and hold me,
   Oh, Holy Spirit.
I offer You
   my heavy, hurting, aching heart.
For my grief is like a valley deep
   with dark caves in which I hide.
My tears blur all my vision.
My pathway goes in circles.
Each circle's filled with pain.
There seems no map for sorrow.
And, Lord,
   I've lost sight of my tomorrow!

Hold fast, my dear disciple.
Love claimed you long ago.
Your grieving
   is My squeezing,
   the pressure of My hand.
A touch that knows
   your sorrow.
A touch that heals today,
   that seals,
   reveals tomorrow.

BWS

CHAPTER FIVE

GRACES

OF THE NIGHT

I n January of 1968, a hysterectomy depleted Betty's waning strength. It was the straw that broke the camel's back. She had no energy or appetite and was experiencing shortness of breath and headaches so severe that she totally lost her ability to focus or concentrate. She became more and more incapable of functioning and was struggling just to get a meal together. Often, she would just stand in the corner and cry. One afternoon, Bryant came in and dropped some invitations to a tennis tournament he was hosting on her desk and told her to address them. When he came back to check on her progress, he found her sitting there staring blankly at the wall, her hand shaking so badly that she couldn't hold the pen. Something finally clicked in him and he called his brother, a doctor, for help. They told Betty they wanted her to go to the hospital in Gainesville for a thorough physical checkup. She didn't resist.

She could have stayed in that depressed place forever; many people do. Fortunately for her, though, the pressures in her world were so strong that she lost even the ability to cope, so she submitted to what they told her to do. She was drowning in her exhaustion, but she knew what she had been doing wasn't working and something had to change. She had no idea who Betty Skinner was; she only knew that she was not who those around her expected or needed her to be. She was unable to function and felt she could not possibly live another day. At forty-two, she hit the bottom of the pit of despair, and that is where the healing began.

Suffering
like water flowing
etching its way through sand and rock
and so in me.
Suffering leaves its mark
as it slowly, painfully
etches its way
through my calloused heart.

"Living with depression is a horrible way to live because it is a living death. It felt like a twenty-pound weight had been strapped on my back and I just couldn't get it off. Nothing excited or challenged me. I couldn't sleep. I lost my appetite because food lost its flavor. I couldn't concentrate. I would pick up a book but couldn't read it; I just held it. It was a tremendous struggle just to exist. Those closest to me couldn't help because they felt very threatening, so I pushed them away. I withdrew into a void of nothingness, which is the pit of despair — the weight of depression.

"For me, the movement toward healing required a complete surrender. God is always saying to us, 'If you will give Me everything, I will give you everything.' It is a constant coming, a constant offering, a constant struggle to let go in order to move to a deeper communion with God. I knew my life was out of control and I needed to change because what I was doing wasn't working. So I quietly packed my suitcase and didn't take a single spiritual book with me, not even my Bible. I somehow knew that I needed to put them down because, strange as it seems, they had become my addiction and, as with all compulsions, were separating my heart from the heart of God.

"When I packed my little blue bag to go to the hospital, I said, 'All right Lord, I've been reading about what a good Christian woman should do and how she should live her life, but I want to say to You, Lord, that it's not working for me. You promised me joy. You promised me peace. You promised me wholeness, and I'm not experiencing any of this. My life is a total disaster. There's got to be another way. I do not doubt Your promises, but I don't understand how to find them.'"

APRIL 23, 1968

I leave today for the hospital in Gainesville. I am emotionally and physically spent.

With great difficulty I have now laid aside all things sent from God that would involve me in any way in His work. A severing can never be halfway; it has to be complete. So for me this means everything — reading, writing, witnessing. As for prayer and meditation, this much I think God will allow if it does not impose on or impair in any way the lives of those around me. My struggle comes now in going and giving where He calls me to go and where He calls me to give.

I am deeply involved with God in my subconscious. We are one. I in Him and He in me. His love, His way of thinking, are mine now and will be forever. This can never be reversed nor would God want it to be. I can take Him with me wherever I go and give Him (Love) away wherever I am.[1]

In conclusion then, I share in depths of

feeling and understanding these thoughts from Bonhoeffer, "Bewilderment is the true comprehension. Not to know where you are going is the true knowledge. My comprehension transcends yours."[2]

Betty sat rigid and immobile in the front seat of the car, locked away from life, drowning in fear that was squeezing her so tight she was literally fighting for every breath. Her head was pounding mercilessly while Bryant, the biggest stress in her life, drove on in total silence for the entire hour and a half to the hospital. It took everything in her to keep from jumping out of the car while it was moving and ending it all. It wasn't the first time she had contemplated suicide, and it was just the grace of God that she didn't do it.

Such anxiety
can I survive, God?
It presses me
no breath, no life, only pain
ripping at my guts.

They checked into a hotel and went to a restaurant, but she couldn't eat anything. Bryant was such a threat to her, and his energy felt so defeating that she hated even being in the same room with him. That night she never got in the bed but just paced the floor, back and forth, all night long. The next morning Bryant checked her into the ambulatory ward of the hospital and left. She could have walked out, but she stayed because she was at last ready to take the first critical step toward healing—admitting she was sick and desperately needed help to get well.

"I really thought I had something physically wrong with me. I would have even settled for cancer at that point if you could just name it. They did extensive tests on me for what felt like a hellish eternity. Finally, Dr. Hart came in and said, 'Betty, we've run all these tests, and I want to assure you that there is nothing wrong with you physically. You have an emotional problem. I can only describe it as sort of a hole in your soul.' I had no idea what he was talking about. I didn't even know what an emotional problem was. That's how far away I was from any inner sense of knowing who Betty Skinner really was."

By getting out of her stressful environment, Betty would have a much better chance to improve because she wouldn't have to use her energy to fight the fear of the world of her reality. Knowing this, the doctor gave her three options: She could take a long trip, she could enter herself into a year-long treatment program at a well-known psychiatric hospital in Connecticut, or she could check into the psychiatric ward there on the eighth floor. The trip appealed to her more than anything, but she knew that wasn't realistic because she was already experiencing a great deal of confusion and disorientation. The longevity of the other hospital program felt overwhelming. The choices were so devastating and her mind so muddled that she couldn't decide, so she asked the doctor what he would recommend. He suggested that she enter the program there. A few minutes later, completely alone, she walked up to the eighth floor and checked herself into the psychiatric ward.

There are a lot of people who love me.
But in my times of deep despair
I am alone.
God, where are You?
Would You caress me
just for a moment
to keep my heart from breaking?

Betty was in such a state of despair and hopelessness that the impact of her illness on her children didn't even occur to her. Bryant agreed with her decision but was totally unaccustomed to the responsibility of caring for children and a household, so he sent Betty's nephew, Pidge, home and made arrangements for Charlie, Betsy, and Russell to go to a boarding school. Bryant Jr. was already away at college. He didn't tell them that their mother had had a nervous breakdown; he just told them she was sick. Everyone in their social world quickly found out that Betty had gone to a psychiatric hospital but she didn't care. She was much too sick to think about anyone or anything other than survival. Even though Bryant was in debt at that point, the huge expense didn't matter to him; he just knew he needed some help. Annie Tartt was no help because she was so trapped in denial that she couldn't emotionally deal with the situation and never even visited Betty in the hospital. It was a terrible time for the whole family.

"Checking into the hospital was the most humiliating experience of my life; it was the place where 'the big I' died. The first thing they did was lock the door behind me and strip-search me for drugs or anything I might use to hurt myself. They were short on beds, so I was put in a ward with several other patients, many of whom were waiting to be transferred to the state mental institution. There was always this scratching at the walls and moaning and groaning going on. I was experiencing such incredibly intense anxiety that I couldn't sit still and could barely breathe. The first night in that place I didn't sleep at all; I could only hold on to the side of the bed and rock—all night long. The overwhelming amount of fear and anxiety got me into this endless rocking motion to release the tension. My whole focus—my only focus—was on survival."

> *Down, down, down!*
> *Is there no bottom*
> *to this endless pit?*
> *this pit of hell?*
> *Darkness, despair, fear*

engulf me.
Please! Please! God!
Hear my crying!

"In the morning they had to force us get to up because no one wanted to get out of bed. We all wanted to stay there and pull the covers over our heads. On top of that, the physical examination the day before had been not only humiliating but painful, so I was very tired and not the least bit hungry. I was just . . . ready to die. I was already dead, bottom line.

"We were told what we could and could not do, eat and not eat, when to go to bed and when to get up, and all the while people stared at us, assessing our every move. We had no freedom; we had no choices. It was a prison and I fearfully surrendered to it. I was fortunate, though, to still have just enough inner light to realize that if I didn't take responsibility for my own life, nothing would ever change. I saw people there who were even worse off than I was, and it was frightening enough to motivate me to get well. My sense was that if I refused to submit to what my family and friends could clearly see I needed to do, I would never get better; I would get much, much sicker."

I am confined within manmade walls.
Suffering and heartache engulf me.
Yet for a priceless moment there is peace
as my thoughts drift to the beauty of the sea
and I seem to be tossed
heedlessly by its waves.
Their foam crested tops are so gentle.
They seem to embrace me
with a special caring and a special love.
The sea is from God.
Perhaps this is His way of caressing me.
Someday I'll be free to go there.

Illumination

Nothing is as debilitating to our spiritual life as fear. It imprisons us, paralyzing our potential to receive the love God so longs to give us. Everyone has fear, but the good news is that we do not have to stay trapped in it. We have a promise: "Perfect love drives out fear"(1 John 4:18). We have a command: "Don't be afraid" (Matthew 10:31). Our work is to believe the promise and be obedient to the command.

We were created with the capacity to move against the negative energy of fear. We all have places of fear inside us but we have other places, too, deeper places of faith and trust and love. As we dare to step out into those places, offering up our fear and opening to receive God's love, trusting that He will meet us, our inborn fear becomes a gift that slowly leads us from its negativity to a new place of freedom and a new kind of fear—a reverent fear that leads to deeper trust in the awesome power of God to heal us.

Every energy that we have can be redeemed by God's transforming love. Nothing that is a part of us ever goes to waste. Even negative fear can be redeemed by love. He changes our natural fear from one that paralyzes to one that liberates and becomes an ally for life and living. That fear and love belong together within us may be difficult to grasp, but fourteenth-century saint Julian of Norwich assures us that it must be this way. "Love and dread are brothers. They are rooted in us by the goodness of our Maker, and they shall never be taken away from us without end."[3] Reverent fear humbly recognizes the lordship and fatherhood of God, and love acknowledges God's goodness. This reverent fear then becomes sweet awe for the transcendent lovingkindness of God that leads us to trust and obedience, and from there to joy and the peace that passes understanding.

Prayerfully, might we approach our lives with reverent fear, trusting that this will bring us to the sweetness of God's love, fearful of only one thing, that we might miss His unspeakable goodness.

Don't be afraid,

Betty

Oh God, gentle first Truth,
*   move in my heart.*
Illuminate each dark corner
*   where webs of self still hide.*
Show me Whose I am
*   that I might know who I am.*
Then recreate me,
*   dress me in Yourself*
*   whose virtue is love,*
*   whose knowledge is truth,*
*   whose beauty is creation.*

Oh God, eternal first Truth,
*   You who created me in love*
*   and longs to re-create me in mercy,*
Bring me to the foot of the cross,
*   To the nailed feet, the gift of Your Son*
And there, in His shadow,
*   In unspeakable gratitude,*
Enable me to live consistently
*   the endless dynamic*
*   of knowledge and love*
*   of gentle first Truth.*

BWS

CHAPTER SIX

STIRRING
SHADOWS

Depression is an emotional disease that comes in many forms; you either cure it or it will get worse. I knew I couldn't straddle the fence. I couldn't continue to just cope. To cope means to get by, to make it through the day. In today's world it might mean you take another pill or read another book or have another drink, but you don't have a handle on anything that will help you get well. You are just coping. The Christian culture might say, 'Look at that poor man, he drank five pints of liquor today,' but it might just as well say, 'Look at poor Betty, she read five religious books today!' I was still just coping. I was still fragmented. I was still depressed. I was still emotionally sleeping. There was no light in my life. It was all dark. Just one more day, please, in this darkness. That's what coping is: one more day in the darkness.

"I thought a lot about the story of Jesus at the pool of Bethesda. In my mind, I saw Him walking slowly toward me among all of those sick people. They all believed that if they could get into that water, they could be healed. He stepped over many people and would stop and speak quietly to others, but I couldn't hear what He was saying. As He got closer, I could see the tears in His eyes. Like the crippled man Jesus spoke to by the pool, I had been lying there for forty years, full of excuses for why I couldn't move to healing. When He finally came to me, He said, 'Betty, do you want to get well?' and I said, 'Yes, Lord.' Then He took my hand and said to me very tenderly, 'I will give you the strength. Now take up your bed and walk. Do your work.' I was mercifully being brought to a choice between life and death. It was severe mercy, but it was sweet, and I chose life."

In 1968, there were very few antidepressants and those that were available were extremely potent. Oddly, the doctors never prescribed any medication for Betty. They undoubtedly would have if she had stayed there much longer, as they were experimenting with new drugs. She was very aware of the fact that when pill time came, the lines would form very quickly. The patients seemed to become dependent on the medications, and watching it made her commit to herself to be very careful about any pills she took.

"I was very fortunate that I was able to get well without having to take any medications. In today's world, the medication situation seems to be spiraling out of control because our culture is so geared to stopping the pain at any cost. We are all created differently; every journey is different, so by all means, if you need the medication, take it and be grateful. It is a gift like everything else and can be very helpful in getting you to a place where you can begin to do the work you need to do to get well, but try to find the balance. Once the medication has gotten you to an even level, it is very important to incorporate physical, mental, and spiritual exercise into your recovery work, because this will treat the underlying problem. This is excruciatingly hard to make yourself do, and progress feels interminably slow. I know; I have been there. I want to assure you though that you can do it, and, if you persevere, the payoff is unspeakably sweet. God is working in you and everything will be all right, but it will take time. The depression will not defeat you."

Why are You so severe, Lord?
Don't You know my loneliness?
The aching abyss of my heart?
My hunger for a smile, a touch, for understanding?
Yes, it is I.
Come unto Me.

The staff tried to keep the patients occupied and exercising, but at that time physical activity was not considered to be much of a factor in one's recovery. An orderly would take them down to a small, dank gym in the basement where they would do the Royal Canadian Air Force exercises. There was also a recreation room with a few old, faded sofas at one end. There were no books because the patients were so depressed they simply couldn't concentrate enough to read. On one side was a door that led outside to a reinforced steel, cagelike enclosure with punching bags hanging by chains from the wire ceiling. A glass bubble at the far end of the room was where the doctors and nurses sat to observe the patients. Occupational therapy consisted of painting precast pottery at a sticky, old picnic table in the corner. Betty painted a small duck, which she still has today. "It was a cute little duck. I painted the darn thing, and I never let it go because it reminds me of those days and my struggle."

Would not death be better
than this aimless wandering?
Such an endless struggle
against despair and fear
like staying afloat in a current
that deprives you of any chance to refill.
Can I survive?

Dry river bed
Parched and empty
Crusty mud, damp sand.
Will the water ever flow again?
Refilling, refreshing,
Silent, clear and cool.

"We went to therapy with a psychiatrist three times a week and group therapy once a week. For me it was staggering, because for the first time in my life I heard people expressing emotions that I thought only I was feeling. When I was in the depths of my depression, I had a sense that no one else in the world could possibly have experienced what I was experiencing or could possibly identify with it. It was so good to know that I was not alone."

After watching her for a few weeks to be sure that she wasn't suicidal or, as she says, "taking alcohol," the doctors decided to allow her to go out of the hospital some during the day. She desperately wanted to get out of that sterile ward and breathe some fresh air, but just getting out of the bed and putting on her shoes was a titanic struggle. Initially, a nurse had to put them on for her, but she persevered, enduring the humility.

"The pain got so bad for me that I put on my tennis shoes and started walking. I walked and walked and walked. I can remember stopping on a little bridge that crossed over a creek. I was holding onto the rail, looking down at the water, feeling so desolate and alone and then, just for a moment, I became aware of a warm Presence in the midst of my pain. It was a tiny flicker of light in my darkness and I clung to it for dear life.

"It's interesting to me now that the doctors didn't encourage my walking or any other natural means of healing. They didn't discourage it, but they sure didn't encourage it. I could feel the difference, though, almost immediately. I would come in from a long, long walk and take a hot shower and feel much better. When I got out of the hospital, I kept the walking regimen and it helped my recovery tremendously."

Ever waiting
to brighten the darkest day
hope
like a patch of brilliant blue
breaks through
the endless mass of gray.

Bryant, in his own way, was trying to be supportive. He couldn't begin to understand the depths of Betty's illness, but he was frightened and did what he could to reach out to her. His willingness to come down to the hospital once a week for marriage and individual counseling said to her that he cared. Through therapy, he learned more about her disease and agreed to do what he could to assist in her recovery. Together, they made choices that strengthened their commitment to each other. Nevertheless, she was still very withdrawn and anxious whenever he came to visit. Just the sound of his voice still triggered enormous pain.

"I was not looking forward to spending our twentieth wedding anniversary together, but I went and ended up having a really nice dinner. He gave me a beautiful ring, but for years every time I looked at that ring it brought back memories of pain. It's okay now, though, because I have learned that when we recall our own pain, we can begin to recall the pain and suffering of Christ, bringing us to a deeper place of gratitude to God and compassion for the suffering of others."

Suffering overcomes suffering
When it is shared with Jesus.

The hospital provided Betty with the time and space to begin to slowly grapple with the vital piece that was still missing in her life: the inner journey. Up to that point, she had had some sense of upreach (the longing to move toward God) and some sense of outreach (the desire to serve others in love), but she had very little sense at all about inreach (the emotional dimension of her life). This is what suffering would teach her. She very gradually began to sense a little bit of freedom as she woke up to her inner life.

Along with this glimpse of freedom came the beginning of renewed creativity for her. We were created in the image of God the Creator and our unique expression is crucial to God's design for the healing of the world. Depression had caused this part of her mind to become almost nonexistent, and its awakening and development were integral parts of her healing. Her slow walk to wellness began by choosing to do those things that enhanced and awakened her senses. The simple act of paying attention to the warmth of the water on her skin when she showered was helping her wake up to her outer senses: taste, touch, sight, sound, scent. This helped her wake up to her inner senses: imagination, memory, and will. All of these things fed her creativity and enlarged her capacity to connect with the divine Creator.

Writing down her thoughts in what she called "little meditations" became Betty's particular creative outlet. The little jottings were crude in the beginning, but as she continued to try to embrace and express her pain and open herself to the Holy Spirit's leadings, her meditations became deeper and more beautifully expressive.

"I remember the first time I realized that I was getting better. I had been in the hospital for almost three months, it was in the summer, and I had gone for a walk. I decided that my room needed some life, so, because I couldn't pick the hospital's flowers, I picked some greenery and put it in the little jars I had decorated in occupational therapy class. I had received quite a few get-well cards, so I pasted them on my walls in a nice little arrangement. It wasn't much but it was a creative expression, and it gave me a sense that I was coming to life.

"As I began to awaken to life and become aware enough to see and say thank you for the tiniest bit of creativity and beauty, I was finding hope for deeper healing and the path to the recovery of my authentic, God-created self. I became more creative as I created and, as my spiritual gifts were refined by the Holy Spirit, my creativity became more pure. My poetry began to flow and it reflected the image of God because it was coming through the pain and the sorrow and the suffering of transformation. This is creative surrender."

The creative mind,
is loving, open, vulnerable.
It is the way out of all limitations,
physical, mental and spiritual.

Illumination

Darkness — with its numbness, loneliness, and shame — very often accompanies a deep spiritual journey and can be the means to the knowledge of both God and self. The freedom to love and be loved is often discovered in the darkness, so it is important to befriend it. We need to view it not as something bad or to be feared but rather as a time of not knowing, a time, not of doing and learning, but of being and unlearning.

If we will look upon this painful season not as the hand of an enemy trying to crush us but endeavor to see it as the hand of a loving God who is closer to us than our breath, leading us down to the ground of our being, our fearsome journey will finally open onto a great, wide plateau of love — a safe place — that abiding place within God. "For in him we live and move and have our being" (Acts 17:28).

To resist, ignore, or reject the hand of such a friendship is to be deaf to the Voice of Love calling us home, the Voice of the Beloved Who created us in love and longs to re-create us in mercy. By submitting to this time of crucifixion and allowing ourselves to be broken by it, we create an opening through which God's love can pour in and illuminate our illusions, liberate us from attachments, and fulfill our heart's desire to discover our true self hidden with Christ.

Remember and be encouraged: "The light shines in the darkness, and the darkness has not overcome it" (John 1:5, RSV).

I love you with His heart, which is soft because it has been broken.

Betty

Beloved, embrace me
in the dark night
of my praying,
in the deep silence
of my offering,
in the confrontation
of my dying.

Beloved, enable me
by faith
to know You without seeing You,
by hope
to possess You without feeling
Your presence,
by love
to desire You above all desires.

Beloved, grant
that I might put
all faith in love for You,
all hope in love for You,
to know that
all desires fail but one:
my desire to be loved
by You.

BWS

CHAPTER SEVEN

GLIMMERS

OF LIGHT

And now go in peace.
Rest in your waiting.
It takes a while to heal,
for strength to come again
after Satan's unrelenting torments.

At the end of four grueling months in the summer of 1968, Betty was well enough to leave the hospital. The doctors knew the patients could become too comfortable in the hospital and sensed this was happening with Betty, so they felt that it was time for her to leave. She was still very depressed and not yet ready to go home, so they decided she needed an interim place to gradually transition back into the real world. A friend provided her with a house not far from the hospital.

So Betty collected her few belongings and carefully packed them in the same little blue bag she had brought to the hospital. She put in the little painted duck, the vases she had made, the cards she had received, and her few items of clothing. Then she put her bag and the plants she had received into a grocery cart they provided for her and rolled it down to the front desk to check herself out. She was very anxious about the checking out process because no one was there to help her, but she managed to sign the papers and roll her cart out to the circular driveway in front of the hospital to wait for Bryant. They drove out to the simple, little white concrete-block cottage that would become the setting for her next stage of healing. It sat at the far end of a shady, clay road that led to a spring-fed lake with a white sand beach in the rolling green horse country of central Florida.

"I had seen the house before. Bryant and I had spent the weekend there with our friends, Ed and Mamie Clark. When we arrived, they were there waiting to welcome me and show me around but left very soon after. I will never forget opening the refrigerator and finding the few little dishes Mamie had left there for me to eat. I thought it was the sweetest thing that had ever happened to me. You see, I had been living in a culture where everything was demanded of me and here someone had done something for me without even asking for a thank you. It really affected me. Later, after Bryant left, I made my bed and walked down to the lake. I just sat there on the beach listening to the water for what must have been hours."

The fear of getting worse and having to go back into that hellish place of darkness and fear motivated her to do whatever it took to get well. Every day, she would walk down to the lake and go for a swim in the cool, clear water. She managed to go to town by herself to buy groceries and even cook her own meals. It took a great deal of time to do the simplest of tasks, but each day brought just a bit more hope, little glimmers of light. Her concentration was coming back slowly and she could read a little bit, but she was still a long way from being well.

She began to experience a few of what she calls moments of heightened perception. It might be a beautiful sunset, a stranger's smile on her walk to town, or the sound of a child's laughter over the lake. In the past, she failed to see these kinds of things, but now when she was given these moments, she would stop and pay attention. She would listen to them and stay with them as long as she could and write about them in her journal. All of this was strengthening her spirituality by taking her outside of herself. She was waking up to the mystery and the beauty and the wonder.

*Out from under
the deep dark night of depression,
the endless weight of it,
a ray of light.
Grab it.
Cling to it.
Fight for it.*

"These little glimpses of beauty and healing gave me the hope and the courage to keep going. I was beginning to feel comfortable in my own skin for the first time in my life. It was so simple, but it was the most tremendous thing I had ever experienced. I wasn't feeling so guilty and inadequate anymore. I was experiencing a tiny bit of freedom from my prison of fear, and it was just enough of a crack in the prison door to keep me moving toward wholeness. Slowly, I began to claim for myself more love from God, which is the key to all freedom. I was moving away from the fear that I was so bound up in toward the Love.

"So much of this required a willingness to wait in my pain and keep watch for the Light. In the story of Lazarus, Mary and Martha waited in their terrible pain and sorrow when their brother died. When He heard of His dear friend's death, even Jesus waited. He stayed where He was for two more days because His Father had not yet told Him to go. So Jesus finally went and when He was just outside the village, Martha and Mary came running out to Him in tears. Scripture says Jesus, the Light of the World, cried with them. He had them take away the stone that was sealing Lazarus' grave, and giving thanks to His Father, called out in a loud voice for the dead man to come out. When he heard Jesus' voice, Lazarus slowly woke up and struggled out of the tomb into the brilliant day. Jesus then told his friends to unbind him and set him free (see John 11:1-44).

"In my own healing, I had to wake up from the deadened state I was in and listen for His voice, let go of the things that were keeping me bound, and be vulnerable and open to however He wanted to heal me. If there was to be any hope for a second chance at life, I had to press through my paralyzing fear, denial, and illusions and slowly find my way home to rest in God. This surrender—this great yes to God—was very difficult. It was a long process, and I only endured it by viewing the suffering I was experiencing as a close and holy darkness and, by grace, holding on to that glimmer of hope.

"God was saying to me, 'Betty, now that you have found a bit of ground to stand on, what choices are you going to make?' When I went into the hospital, I was struggling just for breath, but now I was at a place where I could actually make choices about my commitments. I had some very big choices to make. Would I stay in the marriage? I still wanted to run, to be honest with you. You don't forget that pain too quickly, and you don't want to experience it again, either. I knew I still had a lot of work to do on myself and in the relationships around me, but I was beginning to take heart again and feel the strength to start over. There was a clear enough space in my head to actually connect a thought, evaluate it, and choose what I wanted to do. And I was choosing life. That's just grace."

If you will be obedient, patient and listen
I will prepare you for the vision
I have poured into your heart,
but in My time not yours.
You can do nothing. I must do it all.

To make that choice for life, Betty had to be willing to let go of her old ways. Like a trapeze, as the second bar swung toward her, she had to be willing to release the first bar in order to grab hold of the other. The fearsome part for her — and for all of us — was the little never-never land of empty air between the bars that she didn't understand and couldn't control. This is where most of us lose our courage. So we live out our lives clinging white-knuckled to the same old bar. Betty knew that if she refused to let go of that bar and change, she would never grow, and if she stopped growing, she would never be well or find her true self. So she dared to release the old bar and travel through the never-never space to grab the new bar, and God met her there. His Spirit began to fill her with His love and show her a new way.

"In order to change and grow toward wholeness, I had to get comfortable with mystery. Mystery is that place beyond rational knowing and beyond our capacity to control; therefore, its acceptance felt like a fundamental assault on my way of protecting myself in the world. I had tried to force God into a nice, neat little box of my own construction in order to feel safe and in control of my life, but when I was clinging to my opinions and illusions, I wasn't able to see Who God really was or grow into the fullness of Christ's love. I was so afraid to let go, but I put down my emotional security blanket in order to move back to an open, childlike trust in God — however He chose to reveal Himself."

Blessed Love
encompass me.
Pour Yourself over me.
Love
lift me up
and make me whole.

After a couple of weeks, she was able to have a few visitors. One or two of her children or another family member would come down to the lake for the day, but they were still very threatening to her. Sometimes she would catch herself slipping away from them and sneaking back to the safety of her little room. Her fearfully familiar, obsessive need for privacy and solitude had not yet died.

After a month there, Bryant told her he wanted her to come home. The little cottage had become a place of security for her so she didn't want to leave, and she definitely didn't want to go back into the fire at home. The doctors told Bryant that it would be best for her if she didn't go back to the house she associated with so much pain and stress, but he decided against their advice for the time being. He had a lot invested in that community and wasn't ready to leave. In spite of the anxiety she felt, Betty knew it was time to go, so she went, not knowing what her future held but trusting the One who held it.

"When Bryant came to pick me up, I felt the same old anxiety and intense fear rise up within me. I was far from well but healing is a painfully slow process. There were many, many times when I slipped back into my old, destructive patterns and negative feelings. At least for now, though, I had the courage to go home and trust that God's grace would sustain me there."

You must prepare now for the crowded places.
The lonely quiet places:
beach and mountain,
lake and meadow,
will come later.
The crowded places are difficult.
I know that.
But I will go with you.

Illumination

Nothing on our spiritual journey is ever final; it is an ongoing process moving us deeper and deeper. It is a continuous change and movement from what is good (that place where most of us live, desiring to love and serve God) to what is better (an open and intense desire to hear God) to what is best (when all of our prayer becomes service and all of our service becomes prayer). Most of us stay in the good and never attain the better or the best because the inner work of change is so difficult, our fears are so great, and there are so few to love us and guide us there.

In Luke's gospel, Jesus comes to visit His dear friends and finds Mary and Martha busily making dinner preparations. Mary immediately leaves the work to go and sit at Jesus' feet. Martha, in exasperation, says to Jesus, "Lord, don't you care that my sister has left me to do the work by myself? Tell her to help me!" Jesus' answer to her was, "Martha, Martha . . . you are worried and upset about many things, but only one thing is needed. Mary has chosen what is better, and it will not be taken away from her" (Luke 10:40–42). It is helpful to see that there was nothing wrong with Martha's work; it was good. The tragedy was that her focus was so limited. If she had been lovingly attentive to the awesome reality of the presence of God with her in her work, she would have been able to serve those around her in love and peace without resentment.

The gift that Mary, the contemplative person, offers to Martha, the active person, is the call to slow down and experience the beauty that is present in each moment. "Please, Martha, stop long enough to listen, to pray, to make a little space in your life for God. Go sit by the window for a minute; go take a quiet walk; go anywhere you can and sit quietly and listen." Mary had chosen the better part, but it still wasn't the best. She had not yet learned to take her loving attention into the work that needed to be done. If Mary had taken the love she was receiving from Jesus and graciously offered it to Martha through service, she would have stilled the conflict Martha was feeling and brought peace to the situation.

Mary and Martha represent the conflict we all live with. When we are out of balance in either of these two ways of living, our relationships and our spiritual lives suffer. The Mary in us has to be redeemed through our willingness to become servants in places where we may be very uncomfortable, the world of our reality. If we don't take our spirituality into the real work we are called to, nothing will ever get done. The question for the Martha in us is, "Can I do this work without feeling put upon or resentful but in love and gratitude?" That happens when we finally realize that our transformation requires that we bring loving attention and a sense of the abiding Presence into our work.

It takes the work and energy of a redeemed Martha to do God's work in the world, and it takes compassion flowing through the redeemed Mary to draw people into the community of love. Our prayer is coming to receive this love, and our action is going out to offer it to the hungry hearts of others. When this happens, all of our service becomes prayer and all of our prayer becomes service, and we are never out of communion with Love. This is the movement toward wholeness — toward the best.

Endeavoring to live in His Love,

Betty

Most generous God, You gave me
memory, understanding and will.
You gave me memory
that I might hold Your blessings.
You gave me understanding
that I might know Your truths.
You gave me will
that I might love
what my memory holds
what my understanding knows.
Take my memory that it may no longer
be filled with thoughts of me.
Take my understanding that it may no
longer cling to so much that is not of You.
Take my will that it may choose always
to remember You, always to see You,
always to love You.

BWS

CHAPTER EIGHT

AWAKENING

DAWN

In returning home, Betty was walking back into the world that had triggered the dismantling of so much of her false self. She was beginning to see, though, that the discovery of her authentic self—the true self that God created but remained hidden from her—demanded such disassembling. She longed to be free from the protective walls she knew she had constructed around her heart in a desperate attempt to find security, esteem, power, and control. As she became aware of these illusions, she began to surrender them and was slowly led to a far deeper place of healing and wholeness.

It was a brilliant fall day but the house felt shadowy and threatening as she stepped unsteadily back over the threshold of that place of pain. It was cold and oddly empty because the older children were away at college and the younger two had been temporarily sent to a local boarding school. The eerie quiet was suffocating as she moved slowly through the old familiar rooms. She was terrified and still very depressed but determined to get well, so she willed herself to speak up and say to Bryant that she thought she would be able to handle living there again. She desperately wanted to be able to support him because she was still feeling guilty about all he had gone through with her illness. He was at the height of his career, and she knew how hard it would be for him to leave the community he had risked so much to develop. For his part, he was being as supportive of her recovery as he felt he could be by moving all of the club activities out of the house and by doing his best to simplify things for her. There was so much about her depression, though, that would always remain foreign to him and so much about her spiritual growth that he would never understand.

"It was my choice to go back to that place full of painful memories; no one was forcing me, which is important. It was a sad house, a sad story, a sad place. I must say, I was glad when we finally sold it. I think of all the fun and joy we could have had there but, because of the depression and the fear, it was never a home; it was just a house. Love makes a home.

"I didn't know this then, but I know it now: We must be willing to bring our spiritual life down into the difficult world of our reality because this is our refining fire.

"I had always felt this draw from God, and now I had a strong determination to live and respond to that call. So I decided to stay in the fire and get well. Here I was, this little introverted, broken, depressed, pitiful, forty-three-year-old woman trying to become whole. How could I put this all together? How could I live and be God's person and still survive the world of my reality? Was I going to choose life or was I going to choose death? I knew it was up to me, and I believed that I could choose life because of the encouragement I felt from the few pain-free moments God had mercifully given me. I had never felt that before and those little glimpses of light and freedom gave me hope. Now where this choice would lead, I didn't know, but I knew it was a step away from death toward life. I felt God saying to me, 'Come as far as you can and I will meet you there.' So that's what I did—I began to step into life one day at a time."

Sweet Love,
My dearest Treasure,
I feel the movement in Your prayer,
The intensity of Gethsemane,
The pain of Calvary, Your passion,
The agony You suffered there.
Drops of sweat, a flood of tears
Have touched my hair,
Have washed the wrinkles of my days,
Have set my heart ablaze.

As Betty says so often, "When the teapot explodes, it scalds everything around it." She had slowly begun to recognize the extent of her children's suffering and very much wanted to grow in her capacity to meet them in love. They had been deeply wounded by her absence and inability to meet them in a nurturing way, so each of them acted out their pain differently. She hadn't been able to offer them or anyone else authentic love free from her need to protect and control. She was so fearful, and that fear had kept her disconnected from the Source from which true love and freedom flows. Now, very intentionally and prayerfully, she began to try to reconcile each relationship. That process was long and hard and she continually failed. One morning, as Russell was leaving for school, she was so unkind to him that she felt compelled to go to the school to apologize. He was, of course, mortified when his mother knocked on the classroom door and asked to speak to him. Nevertheless, she was trying, and God honored that.

It took a long time for the children to realize that their mother was finally well and whole enough to have a relationship with them. She very slowly began to function more normally. She was exercising, cooking meals again, and trying to spend a little time with each one individually as they would allow. God was faithful, though, and very, very gradually they began to try to trust her again and benefit from her healing. Little by little, as the years were to prove, "the Lord returned the years that the locusts had eaten" (Joel 2:25, Betty's paraphrase).

"I was still in a great deal of pain over many things: the guilt of having let Bryant down, the pain of my children, and the fear that I still hadn't worked through; but rather than get bogged down and let the fear and anxiety take over, I would immediately make myself put on my shoes and go for a walk and try to change my focus. I was very aware of doing that. I came again and again and again to His table in prayer trying to refocus and receive the love, and what happened? Everything happened. I began to heal, my family began to heal, and our world began to come together. God started doing the work; I just had to be open to it. God, in His mercy and grace, very, very slowly began to show me a new way. I stepped out in faith and started doing my work."

In acts of love I strayed from truth.
There was no escape. The scrutiny came.
The PAIN.
And deep within, the purging cry,
Why? God, why?
Yet, from this hell, this valley of despair,
I rose to heights I dared not dream
were even there.

"I was beginning to learn a little about authentic love, and God patiently encouraged me with moments of heightened perception. I called them little 'Ahas'—so that's what that means! I remember one day in particular, shortly after I got home. Bryant had this habit of putting his shirt on the bedpost if a button was missing. He wouldn't ask me to fix it; he would just put it there subtly saying, 'Get it done.' Well, that brought out all the resentment and anger in me that I could possibly muster. I had recommitted to the marriage and to learning how to love him, but there I was, pacing back and forth across the room looking at that shirt hanging there and experiencing the depths of negativity. It was just destroying me. I walked over to the sliding glass door feeling absolutely no sense of communion, totally drowning in a downward spiral of negativity when, suddenly, for the first time in my life, I felt the Spirit of God speaking to me. The Voice was saying, 'Betty, you're still not getting it, are you?' I answered, 'No, Lord, I'm still not getting it. I'm a long way from it today. This button thing has really got me down. I can sew the button on but I can't do it in love, there's just no way.' Then the little inner Voice said, 'Betty, let Me tell you something, you are not sewing that button on for Bryant, you are sewing it on for Me.' God was saying to me, 'Get your attention, get your focus, connect with My love,' and it powerfully spoke to me. I can't truthfully say that I was able to sew the button on in love that day, but it was a start and a huge help. If I sew the button on but I'm not sewing it on in love, then I'm just coping; I'm just getting by to please Bryant. I'm not free."

It is not enough
just to overcome.
We must overcome
in the Spirit of Love.
In the restoration of the ruin,
In the completion of the work
we must endure.
We must finish well.
The sweetness of the fruit bears witness
to our faithfulness in the task.
In the strain
we find our strength in Him.

In her pain and confusion, she turned to God and asked for help to stop the incessant flow of negative thoughts. This endless repetition was a fearful, consuming self-preoccupation keeping her from grasping reality, which was in turn hurting her health, her relationships, and her experience of life. Her challenge lay in trusting that all of her reality was good and held exactly what she needed and that every circumstance in her life was perfectly engineered by God in order to draw her closer to Him.

Change
the alteration of one's present course.
Why is it so difficult
to direct ourselves toward uncertainty?
To let go,
to fly free for a moment,
to trust.
God knows this need.
Fall, Winter, Spring
These are His changing things.

Illumination

There is within us all this strong desire for the freedom to live and be whole, but it takes enormous courage and discipline to make the choice to trust God and do the difficult work this requires. Taking those initial steps toward change can be so frightening and painful that we often quit before we have a chance to experience any healing. The old voices in our head tell us it won't work, we'll only get worse, and we're wasting our time. The new Voice in our heart tells us that if we don't change, we won't grow, so dare to let go, trust God and make the choice to change, regardless of how hard it is.

Change and growth are synonymous. We have a choice and our choice is critical because it is either life-giving or life-draining. Failure to dare to change keeps us trapped in old behavior patterns that obviously haven't worked so why not take a chance on trust? Old behavior patterns are so hard to break, because they are deeply rooted in our childhood wounds and like a stubborn weed their thorny vines choke out our life. The more we develop new behavior patterns, though, the easier the work becomes because we slowly begin to see our life bear fruit. We feel better physically, so we begin to feel better emotionally. When we feel better emotionally, our self-esteem and self-confidence begin to spark within us a new desire for life.

In my own work of moving against depression, it took me awhile, but I slowly realized that the very thing I didn't want to do in my recovery work was usually the thing I needed to do. I deeply believed that God would help me get well, but I began to see that, to be well and whole I had to submit and accept the struggle of change. I had to truly trust Jesus as Savior.

The suffering way of Jesus is submission, acceptance, and trust. As Jesus lived, so are we to live, trusting that new life flows out of the choices we make and all that we surrender. It takes a great willingness to choose to surrender all of our sorrows, all of our needs, and all of our fears, and trust the intimate love of a very present God. But if we will choose this descending way of humility, we will find our way to freedom. I know this is so, because I have experienced it.

May the Holy Spirit fill, inspire, and bless you as you make the choice for life.

I remain ever His faithful servant,

Betty

The green has turned to golden.
Some branches bare, their leaves have fallen.
And I, His chosen, come again to ponder,
Within the changing pattern of creation
The beauty in the dying,
The forgiving face of God.
Oh, Good Jesus,
In Your redeeming power,
Liberate my broken, crushed self-image,
Worn, tired, abused and torn.
Refine within me Your kiss of peace
That I might extend to others
Your hand, Your word, Your heart of love.
This unity of forgiveness,
The beauty in the dying.

BWS

CHAPTER NINE

ELUSIVE

HOPE

Betty's recovery continued but not as quickly or as smoothly as she had hoped. When she was finally ready to read again, a book fell into her hands by Christian psychiatrist Paul Tournier called *The Healing of Persons*. She was still struggling with her concentration at that point, so she was just flipping through it, but she hit on the very thing that the Spirit wanted to reveal to her.

Tournier taught her that a whole person consists of three parts: a healthy body, a serene mind, and a powerful spirit. She recognized that she was out of balance in all three of these areas, because she had been out of touch with the Spirit of God who brings us into balance. The world was constantly telling her she wasn't good enough, so her wounded ego was always leading her to places where she could feel successful or in control. As a result, she unconsciously over-focused on the aspect of herself that she felt most competent in, which was her identity as a good Christian woman. She got way out of balance in the spiritual dimension of her life and totally neglected the physical and mental dimensions. On some level she still believed the critical voices in her head that were telling her she was worthless, unlovable, and incompetent, so the areas she could control became a way for her to feel better about herself. These things then began to enslave her as they do all of us.

"Self-hatred, so insidiously embedded in my wounded heart, was the greatest enemy of my spiritual life because it constantly contradicted the Voice within that was calling me His beloved. I never felt worthy. The very nature of the ego is its insatiable desire; it will always want more. So we obsessively exercise or starve our bodies, compulsively seek more academic or financial success or drown ourselves in good works in a frenetic attempt to satisfy that inner critic constantly telling us we are not good enough. I got out of balance by using religious things to cope with my fears and insecurities. They had become my idols and they were destroying me.

"The first thing I realized was that I needed to have a healthy body. I had always thought it was selfish to spend time taking care of Betty, but I was now seeing that one of life's warmest paradoxes is that self-love is not selfish at all. How could I have any energy to love and serve my neighbor if my body was broken down because I had no love for myself? Being a good Christian seemed to me, before my breakdown, to be this exhausting effort to continually meet everyone else's needs, but I realized the hard way that I did not humanly have the strength to sustain this compulsion and eventually burned out. As I connected to the Eternal Fire deep in my soul, I was finally able to stop trying to fix and change everyone and everything. I began to try to simply meet everyone in the love, acceptance, and compassion that I had received from God.

Life consists of three loves:
Love of God,
Love of self
Love of others.

If we are to live fully;
If we are to grow toward wholeness;
If we are to feed the hungry hearts of others
Each love must be learned separately
Then carefully and patiently integrated.

"I was lucky because I had a little more free time now that the children were grown. I realized I had been totally fragmented with unimportant things so, instead of filling what time I had with more busyness and activity, I used it to do my inner work. I believed if I had the desire, God would create the spaces and places for me. Often it meant just giving up one TV program or walking through the woods or getting up the courage to turn down one volunteer request. I realized that, if my life was ever going to speak for God, then I needed to be in balance and each part of my being would have to be individually and carefully nourished. In Luke 2:52, Scripture says that Jesus grew in 'wisdom (mind) and stature (body), and in favor with God and men (spirit).'

"I knew that I needed a very structured approach to my physical healing because failure to do my work would cause me to slip backward, and I knew how difficult that road was. I began to eat healthy food and created a simple exercise discipline that worked for me. I found that it was better to do the most difficult item on my agenda first to get it out of the way or I might not do it at all. Because my body had been so totally neglected, just getting out of bed, putting on my old tennis shoes, and going out to walk was my most difficult challenge, so I did that first. I could only go a very short distance at first, but gradually, I built up my strength to the point that I could walk the 1.7 miles around the lake behind our house. As I began to get stronger, I was able to run that distance. I remember, in 1971, being so excited when I found out that a running shoe designed especially for women had just come on the market. I went right out and bought a pair. The simple discipline of getting out and walking that had seemed so torturous in the beginning became a joy and eventually took me to many magnificent mountain hikes and, unbeknownst to me, to a whole new depth of spiritual experience."

Change.
To let loose the trapeze,
To fly free,
To allow space,
To move, to breathe, to grow.

Betty spent a great deal of time pondering the second piece of Tournier's vision for wholeness, the importance of a serene mind. She knew that Scripture said she had been given the mind of Christ and a magnificent soul made in the image of God. She longed to express that creatively, so she disciplined herself to continue keeping a journal. Her little meditations got more poetic as her physical senses woke up, and she began to see many things with new eyes. The expression of that creativity nourished her soul and enhanced her healing.

"So often I had allowed my compulsions and fears of what people might think to block my creativity. As I was able to let go of all that and allow the Holy Spirit to re-create me, the possibility of unlimited creativity could flow. Creativity is that which was in me that was gift but, in my case, had not been offered because of the fearful limitations I had put on myself. Open heart, open mind. As I opened to the One who created me in love and longed to re-create me in mercy, I discovered the gifts that God had given me for His purposes. What I did with my gifts may not have seemed like much to anyone else, but I wasn't doing it for anyone else anymore. Whether my creative expressions had any literary or artistic merit didn't make any difference. The important thing was that when I was creating, I was losing myself in and expressing myself through something that was uniquely mine. I was simply trying to add my little unique piece to the mosaic that was building the kingdom of God. The gift that this brought with it was the wonderful feeling of freedom. Those moments when I was most creative brought me into deeper communion with God, because I was free of myself just for a little while and I was expressing what I sensed about God. Creativity was very, very healing for me, particularly in working out of my depression."

This opening to creativity and new ways of seeing and hearing the Holy Spirit helped her immensely but she knew she had to go even further by learning to diversify her activities and interests. Diversification is very different from fragmentation. When she was fragmented, she was allowing the demands of her ego and her world to run her ragged, performing under the weight of obligation but in diversifying she was making a deliberate choice to pursue a new interest or area of study in order to develop her God-given intellect and find greater balance in her life.

"All of our married lives, I had been running one way and Bryant had been running the other. He ran compulsively toward the world and I ran compulsively away from it. We had totally different interests and were constantly butting heads. My husband's personality and mine were totally opposite in every way but I know now that God put us together to force me to grow.

"Christ tells us that we are not to come to the altar in conflict, so I realized that one of us would have to change. I had learned that love always takes the initiative so I made the choice to try to be more interested in what he was interested in, at the same time diversifying my narrow interests. Bryant is a huge Florida Gator football fan and loves to go to all of the games, but I rarely went with him because I was so depressed. My fear and illusion told me that it was much more important to stay home to rest and have time to myself than to be involved in the shallow activities of the world. I began to rethink all of this and decided that perhaps if I understood the game better I might get more interested in the darn thing. So I signed up for a class to learn about football and soon learned the strategy, the plays, and all of the different positions—tight end is definitely my favorite. The funny thing is, now I'm as big a fan as he is. This may sound like a small thing, but to him it was huge, because he was seeing more life in me and he finally had a partner again. To me it was much more than even that; it was Christ helping me grow as a person and loving Bryant through me."

My times
of work, of play, of rest
they come and go.
And through this intermittent pattern
I learn
the faith, the trust, the love
that sparks the glow
to feed life's appetite
and make it grow.

Betty could see that she didn't have anything close to what Tournier called a powerful spirit, so she committed more deeply to the difficult choice she had made going into the hospital to put down all things "religious" for a while to try to create the space to hear from God. Instead of being a means of finding or opening to God, they had been her security blanket and means of escape from her frightening and stressful world. So she picked up the phone and told all of her church and ministry groups that she just could not be there any more. She didn't try to explain anything or defend herself, she just trusted God with their response and didn't look back. For her, the sedative for emotional pain had been hiding in Christian books and good works, but they were really only deadening the pain; they were not healing it. This was a behavior pattern that she would have to confront again and again and again.

As she integrated all of these areas in her life more and more, she slowly began to develop a genuinely powerful spirit. She had tasted suffering, had been mercifully graced to enter its pain, and allowed herself to be broken by it and re-created by God. She began to trust that her daily activities were not a series of random events; rather, they were God's way of teaching her about her deepest self. She accepted her inability to heal herself and in so doing, mysteriously surrendered her compulsions, illusions, attachments, and cultural conditioning to the healing love of God. This process took an enormous amount of time and required simplifying her external life, turning off her old voices, and waking up to her inner soul life.

"As I made all these changes in my behavior and thinking, I had this picture in my mind that helped me understand better what I was doing. It was as if my life were a kite string that had gotten all tangled up in a ball of knots. The knots were the illusions I was living, the labels I had put on others and myself, the need I had to control others and protect myself, the voices of my cultural conditioning, and everything else I was clinging to. If I was ever going to get well, I needed to let all of that tangled string out a little at a time and then, very slowly and carefully, bring it back in straight each time a new truth was revealed to me. That process went on for years; it didn't happen overnight. When I experienced what I called a little lightbulb truth, I would try to trust it and live it out, allowing the string to untangle just a little more.

"I so strongly believed these truths I was hearing that I acted on them, which was critical. If I hadn't acted on the ones I was given, I don't think God would have given me many more. I would have stayed stuck where I was and God couldn't have taken me on to the next step. These little lightbulbs were a huge encouragement and sustained me in the difficult world of my reality: the place where God had put me. I began to realize, too, that this world was the place of my purification and transformation, so rather than be depressed about it, lost in it, and fearful of it, I began to accept it. It was my life, my choice, my work, and

I needed to take responsibility for it and I didn't need to explain it or tell anyone about it.

"As my perceptions changed, everything around me began to change. It happened very, very slowly, though, because to change my way of thinking and living, I had to return and return and return to the Source to help me find my way. I had to ask over and over for a new way of seeing and reflect on it again and again. God was so gracious and so merciful that I looked back one day and realized that change had begun to happen. Gradually, the physical and the emotional parts of my being began to come together. I was slowly waking up to life. Food began to taste better, my concentration came back, and my relationship with Bryant and the children got better. That doesn't mean that anything or anybody else really changed but I saw them differently because I was seeing with new eyes—God's eyes. These were all broken people, too, and that was okay—I could love them right there."

Illumination

Simplicity is a huge piece in our spiritual journey. Hidden in the center of our being, we all have a beautiful, sacred simplicity that we can discover and live from. It is the child in us created in the image of God before it was wounded by the ways of the world, before it was covered by fear and its darkness, before the Fall. It is our true self.

Again and again, Jesus tells us we must become as little children. It is through silence and solitude that we discover this divine innocence He is calling us back to. A little baby, lying quietly on its mother's breast, hears only her sweet, sweet voice speaking love, joy, and truth. Our journey home is to be born again to that first innocence. This journey is an ongoing process, and all the time we are returning, we are becoming as little children by simplifying, getting rid of the things the world has imparted to us: the false voices, the labels we put on people, our opinions, our illusions, our attachments. Jesus encourages us to go out in childlike simplicity and love, trusting that the gift of ourselves, in Him, is enough.

The great imperative for this interior simplicity is awareness. We must pay close attention to the thoughts that are going on inside of us and how they relate to what we do and who we are becoming. If we will practice quieting the chatter in our minds, our minds finally become absolutely quiet and able to hear the Spirit's voice. In this moment, God is showing us what we must let go of and we don't ask why. We don't doubt. We do it. Any doubt will delete the communion with God that enables us to step out in faith and obey.

As we come to the quiet and do the discipline of intimate listening and obedience to the Holy Spirit, our divine Parent, we will be brought into a simplicity that moves us toward wholeness and holiness. Letting go of our inner chatter and condemning conserves precious energy and opens a space in us that allows the pure love of God to flow into and through us to others.

If we will learn to humbly accept ourselves and others as they are and everything as it is rather than as we wish it were, trusting that because it is, it is good and for our highest good, then we will begin to see that we already have everything we need and that we possess a core place within us of perfect peace, simple trust, and limitless love. It takes courage to claim this simplicity and trust this core, but this is our path to wholeness. So we must continue to come to prayer to hear the Beloved's voice say to us, "I created you. I love you. Your life is an offering and I am giving you the opportunity now to give it for others. Your suffering has been great but it has broken your heart open and filled it with My compassion for the world. It is enough."

Knee bent and full of wonder, might we find every place a place full of God's simplicity, love, and delight.

Betty

O, Beloved of my soul, yet again I come alone
    to seek Your Face, to hear Your Voice, to know Your heart
    in quiet summer days, in endless mountain ways.

O, Beloved of my soul, it's You I so desire.
    Refresh, renew, refill me.
    From morning mist that lifts to pure blue sky
        then hides you, Your mysteries,
        in the silence of the clouds.
    From gentle breeze that stirs the trees
        and moves the leaves against my face.
        It's You, Lord, Your love, Your Grace I feel, I taste.
    From streams of cool, clear water
        immersing me in wonder and in oneness.
        It's You, Lord, Your voice,
        Your song I hear the rapids sing.
    From rock and moss, from earth and flower
        whose very touch is warmth.
        It's You, Lord, Your Fragrance that they bring.
    From evening rapture,
        pink shadows on the mountain face
        lost in the lingering twilight.
        It's You, Lord, Your Presence,
            Your way of saying
                Good night.

BWS

CHAPTER TEN

THE

SILVERY VEIL

Betty put down her spiritual books and activities but she did not put down prayer. Every morning she got up before sunrise and sat quietly with the simple desire to spend a little time alone with God. It was her human effort to make a little space in her life for God. She desperately wanted to learn how to love, so she came empty-handed to the altar and vulnerably opened her heart, as best she could, to what God wanted to show her. She was taking the time to come to prayer to receive the Love so that she would be able to go out into the world and offer the Love. As always, God was faithful and met her right there.

"I was learning very, very gradually to be still and know God as I made the choice to respond to Love. When we are in communion with God, we are drawn into that sweet relationship of love that is going on all the time between the Father and the Son. This is where I yearned to live. As I persevered in prayer, the divine life within me began to wake up and I saw the world with new eyes. I was being re-created from within through the gift of Christ's passion and sacrifice. It was from this hidden place in the

Spirit who is always praying through us that I was going to be able to do the work of transforming my world."

It's not only that our knees are bent,
But rather that our hearts are broken.

Two and a half years later, in 1973, Betty and Bryant sold their house and decided to rent a house a few miles away at the beach until they could decide where they wanted to live. All of the kids except Russell were married or away at college, so they were ready for a smaller place. Betty was still struggling with a few small bouts of depression, so the thought of being able to lose herself in the sights and sounds of the beach was very appealing.

She had been playing a lot of tennis, so she joined the tennis team at the beach. She was one of the best female tennis players in Jacksonville, and the team she captained won the city championship. She was such a good player that she soon found herself out of balance again, this time in the physical aspect of her being. Her identity was still caught up in other people's opinions of her, and tennis was feeding this need. Nevertheless, it was good for her because she needed to rebuild her self-esteem. In the process, she was also finding fulfillment and diversifying her interests by helping Bryant with all of his parties and community and political activities.

"I was waking up now—not fully awake by a long shot—but I was really enjoying playing tennis and feeling good about myself. At the same time, though, I was aware of another movement going on in me. I sensed that I had moved away from that inner echo, the eternal Love call in my life. I knew I needed to get my focus back, regain my spiritual balance, and step out toward God in faith again. To do this, I needed to trust God and let go of playing so much tennis. More and more, I was seeing that trust was tied to obedience. If I sensed Him telling me to do something, I needed to trust Him and do it—no questions asked. If I hesitated, procrastinated, or calculated, I would miss the moment, and that moment in time would never, ever come again. If I couldn't trust Him enough to do what I sensed He was asking, how would my faith ever grow, and how would I ever learn to hear His voice?

"I had to be open to everything if I wanted to grow in the love and knowledge of God. Fear kept me clinging to old habits and old ways of doing things. I had to continually turn off the head tapes that had programmed me for so long and return to my First Love. That required trust and faith — not knowing where I was going but with Whom I was going. Faith brought me to love. Faith brought me to joy. Faith brought me to wholeness. I had to let go of the old trapeze, float through that never-never land, trust God, and grab for the new one. I had to remind myself that God is a God of love and His timing is perfect, so He would not let me fall. That's growth, and all of this led me to a deeper, more vulnerable, more powerful spirit."

> *Not pressed in the mold*
> *or enslaved to pattern*
> *I am a seeker, free,*
> *longing to step beyond*
> *conformity, the conventional*
> *into the ultimate of God's plan*
> *for completeness*
> *my own uniqueness.*

So she put down her racket and trusted God to fill her time. The languid, leisurely months that ensued in the little house on the beach provided a peaceful space for deeper contemplation that enabled her to begin to integrate all that she was learning. The children were pretty well on their own now, her furniture was in storage, so she had no real household duties and had dropped out of all of her volunteer obligations. All of this provided her with time to walk on the beach reflecting on what God was unfolding within her.

Betty was moving into a period in her life that she described as a plateau time, a time when life is relatively peaceful after a tough uphill climb through painfully dark or difficult circumstances. It seemed to her that, too often, when given these quiet periods, people tended to fill up the space with more activity instead of slowing down and breathing in the nourishment of the spacious season. Betty resisted that temptation, using the time, instead, to be with God and do the inner work that would lead her to deeper healing.

"Walking on the beach was helping me get in touch with my senses. Everything was speaking to me. During my depression, I would walk on the beach and hear absolutely nothing, but now, in the sound of the surf, I heard God's voice telling me I was His beloved daughter. I would swim in the ocean and revel in the sting of the salt on my skin, the roll of the waves softly lifting me, and the warmth of the sun enfolding me. Everything was engulfing me. All of my senses were coming alive and I was experiencing God on a deeper level."

The end comes.
Don't hurry.
Take your time.
Close your eyes.
Breathe the air.
Feel the sun.
Know the sand.
Hear the sea.
The sting of salt engulfs me.

"I loved the stormy days. I would sit for hours in the shelter of a little sand dune and watch the power of the ocean. When the surf is rough, it kicks up a lot of foam that glides noiselessly over the sand, moving with the flow of the wind and the water as if it were on ice. It spoke to me of emptiness. The foam didn't care which way the wind blew it—so light, claiming nothing. I watched the sea oats bend with the breeze, and they, too, spoke to me of going with the flow of life—so free, no resistance. They were very top-heavy, yet no matter how strong the wind was or how much turbulence, they bent but never broke; they followed the flow of the wind. You see, I hadn't been going with the flow of life, and I broke. Now I was learning to bend. Everything was speaking to me about God's movement in creation and how I should live my life. It took a long time, but I was beginning to understand that I didn't have to try to change or control my circumstances. God would supply my needs and sustain me in them because He loves me."

Betty was slowly realizing that God had already given her everything she needed. She didn't have to cling. She didn't have to grasp. She didn't have to control. She could totally surrender her heart, her intellect, her emotions, and her will and entrust herself to Love. Her inner life and outer life were beginning to merge in prayer and take her into the freedom and wholeness she had been longing for all her life. She began to live each moment as sacred, unattached, content in whatever it might contain, trusting that she was connected to the Source of love that was always working for her good. The dark, heavy cocoon that she had spun for herself was becoming more and more transparent. Its silvery veil revealed the shadow of the beautiful butterfly hidden within.

A platoon of pelicans,
wings spread
silent, drifting
yet so perceptive
so sensitive
to each movement

of the other.
Through their pattern
seems to flow
a free expression
of unity and trust
of grace.

Illumination

Prayer is simply an offering of our hearts to God, for we truly have nothing more to give. Prayer is where it all begins, and I'm sure it is where it all ends. It is an encounter with the living God. It is descending into the depths of our being to be with Him in the silence and stillness—listening, waiting, and resting. To engage with Him in friendship, in conversation, in thought, getting lost in mystery, lost in wonder, love, and praise is what our journey is all about.

Our quest is simply to know God. This encounter with the living God is what we are hungry for. We have been created by God to need God and have been given an infinite capacity for Him. Our soul is the holy temple within us where Christ lives and where we meet the Divine. As we draw near to God in the hiddenness of prayer, God begins to reveal Himself to us.

In prayer, we are submitting and allowing this encounter with Love to change us. As we look on Love, we are reshaped by Love into the likeness of Christ. The quest to become like Him can happen only when we are with Him. How could it happen any other way? It is the discipline of returning in quiet and stillness and simply being with God that opens this possibility of our transformation. By being still, we are quieting our concern with ourselves in order to be with Him in deep, deep intimacy. This work is difficult because it is hidden, and God's timing and ours are not the same. God is silently at work within us even when we aren't aware of it. The more we intentionally offer ourselves to the Beloved, the more the Love flows in and the more we become like Him.

Gradually, we find our focus. Our will is disciplined, our mind is stilled, our heart is surrendered, Spirit touches spirit, and thus we experience His Presence. We come home to God.

May our heart's desire for God be intensified as we respond to the Love waiting within us, continually coming to Him in prayer.

Betty

Today I walked in God's cathedral,
its stained glass windows
framed in leaves of shapeless wonder
and etched in brilliant tones
of red and greens, of golds and yellows,
then brought to life and set aglow
by streams of sunbeams
flowing from a clear blue sky.

Each tree, grounded in the earth,
stood straight and strong,
free to let its lovely garment go,
its leaves held gently
until the wind came to release them.

I walked amid the whisper of their falling
that broke the silence of my communion
as though it were God's sweet voice calling.

I felt a stirring deep within
a welling up, a tear.
My stony heart was soft, was still;
My soul, God's altar and God's will;
God's glory.
For on this day
CREATION
had told its story.

BWS

CHAPTER ELEVEN

EMERGING

TRUST

After six months, they were ready to find a permanent home. Bryant had always wanted to build a house on the beautiful piece of oak hammock land they owned called The Old Still. Betty said that would be fine with her. The only question she had was where they would live while they were building because there was no house on the property. His answer to that—always the consummate problem solver—was, "I have a trailer and I'll get the bulldozer to pull it down there in the woods and put a little screen porch around it so it'll be nice. We'll just live there and watch the house go up." She had never lived in a trailer before and thought it sounded like an adventure, so they did. He hadn't mentioned that it was a very old, used trailer—not even a double-wide. It was long and narrow like a Pullman car on a train. It was so small Betty could reach around from the bed in the bedroom at the back of the trailer and turn the light on in the bathroom and reach around from the bathroom to turn the light on in the kitchen. Clearly, there was no room for Russell, their only one left at home, so Bryant made a small bedroom for him in what used to be the feed room in the concrete block barn next to the trailer.

There were no windows in it and no plumbing, so Russell had to traipse over to the trailer every time he wanted to use the bathroom.

There was only one really big problem, though, and that was the rats. They would constantly get into the trailer and chew holes in the furniture. Betty laughingly says that was the only time she threatened to leave Bryant, and she actually did leave. She went to her mother's house and told him that when he got rid of the rats, she would come back. He came up with the idea of putting strips of sheet metal at an angle all around the trailer so the rats couldn't climb up and get into the house. Sure enough, that kept the rats from getting in but it also trapped a lot of them inside and they died there. It took him about two weeks to get the trailer cleared out and odor-free enough for her to come back. Other than that, she really did love it out there.

"Bryant set up a special little place outside the trailer under a stand of beautiful trees where he built a huge fire every afternoon. My daughter-in-law called it the eternal fire. That winter the air was cool and fresh as only Florida winters can be, and I would sit there in my old camp chair watching the tiny flickers of fire float up through the leaves of the tall pine trees and vanish into the stars. The sparks singed all of the lower limbs of the trees that winter. Sometimes Bryant or Russell would sit with me, but I remember those times more of being just God and me. It was very, very special. Sitting there with the awareness of feeling and being well was so wonderful. I had felt so horrible for so long that being able to sit by a roaring fire, listening to the logs crackle, smelling the smoke, and feeling the cool air on my face was incredible. It's hard to explain, but when I was depressed all of my senses died: smell, sight, touch, and sound. The fear numbed them. So, in experiencing all of this, I had returned to life.

"The other piece of this was that I was beginning to taste freedom now. I was finding my own voice and no one could press me into a mold anymore. It was startling when I woke up and realized that I had never dared to live out of my own unique truth but from scripts written by my family, friends, church, job, and culture. As I began to wake up and get rid of my illusions, attachments, and those old voices, the little prison I had gotten myself into began to dissipate, and what filled the space? The Spirit of Love, the Spirit of God. I was coming more and more into communion with Ultimate Reality, which is God. God is only in reality. He is not in my illusions. Only in the now—the present moment—can I meet Him and touch His hand. Paradoxically, when we are totally aware of the gift of the present moment, its clarity, beauty, and simplicity are branded into our memory forever to encourage us. By bringing us back to a moment in time when we were immersed in Love, these memories encourage us to continue to trust and let go. So that year He sat me down by the campfire and said, 'I'm going to sit here with you,' and we sat together almost every evening. It was beautiful, and I return there often in my memory."

Emptiness
open, sensitive, receptive
innocence, still and silent,
awaiting a new wholeness
more awesome, more beautiful.
A Stranger refilling me.

"I didn't know at the time why God was putting me out there in the midst of that beautiful solitude, but I melted into it. I could have said, 'I am not staying back here in this rat-infested trailer,' but I had finally gotten to a new place of accepting whatever happened in trust. I know now that I was being given the quiet space I needed to do the work of detaching from old voices and learning to hear what God wanted to teach me.

"God was changing me and I didn't even realize it. I was reading the Bible again and seeing things that challenged some of the beliefs I had accepted without question in my past. I just couldn't see how any human being could tell me how to respond to Christ's love and leading. If

I believed and did only what others told me to believe and do, I was not going to be able to believe and do what God wanted. I committed more and more to the work of prayer, Scripture study, and contemplation in the hope that I might know and experience God as He wanted to reveal Himself to me.

"There were so many things I needed to learn and unlearn, but one of the biggest revelations in my work of recovery was that I couldn't fix or change reality. God is in control of the circumstances of my life and I am simply His person in those circumstances. It took so much negative energy to try to control my reality, and God is not in negativity. I began to see things in myself and other people differently. Instead of looking at the ways that I, in my false self, perceived that Bryant was hurting me, I realized that if I didn't forgive him and love him where he was, I would never heal. I couldn't fix him or change the way he saw me.

"While I was still so trapped in my old compulsions, Bryant and I would get into a conflict, and I would inevitably give in to this tremendous need to explain and justify my behavior. I immediately began to defend myself and rationalize my behavior, denying my part in the problem and seeing him as totally guilty. The minute I started doing that, I stopped listening to him. I finally understood that this was what Bryant was doing too, so trying to defend myself was a huge waste of energy and just throwing kerosene on the fire. This was not love and it was not healing anything. Jesus was perceived as guilty, but He didn't defend Himself. He forgave, so I, too, had to learn to forgive and not defend. I couldn't do any of this, though, until I began to shift my focus from Bryant to the Beloved.

"When we defend ourselves, deny our culpability, or define another person or situation by labeling them, we cease to see things as they really are. A situation that we label as terrible is, in reality, to be used in some mysterious way for our good. We might label a woman a snob because she is so beautiful or successful and we never see her heart. A child might be giving us a difficult time, so we label him 'the problem child' and relate to him that way, never seeing his heart or our part in the problem. That child belongs to God. We need to trust Him to be as creative with our children as He has been with us. We get so caught up in competing, comparing, and controlling that there is no hope of love. Remember that love always takes the initiative so reach back and reconcile.

"Bryant's controlling ways were still stifling me, but now I realized that his excessive need to control was hurting him too. I was the one who had made him my god because I wasn't looking at the real God. Gradually, I began to see Bryant's ways with compassion. He was missing so much that I could have offered him. He needed my unconditional love as much as I needed his, but I wasn't able to give it to him because of the fear I still felt of his power over me. I was ready to pour out love, but his control shut me down. His need was starving us both. It was so clear to me all of a sudden that I came in and wrote down these few little words: 'Control stifles the very life it needs to survive.' It was so simple, but this was another huge piece in my spiritual journey.

"Once I began to wake up and realize that Bryant was not a god, that there was a very real God who loves me and supplies my needs, the fear left. I had been looking to Bryant to supply my emotional needs, and he wasn't able to do that. I had spent far too much time being angry, frustrated, and depressed about it, which only created a downward spiral for me and our marriage. I finally woke up and realized that there was not one thing I could do to change him, but there was an awful lot I could do about me.

"When I began to do my work of letting go of the expectations I was putting on our relationship, it began to mend. Slowly, I began to go with the flow of the circumstances of my life. I could let him do whatever he wanted to do—those were his choices—without being drawn into that familiar vortex of negative, codependent energy. Only God could enable me to see with new eyes and clean up these scraps of the mess of my false self. To do this, I knew I had to stay focused, recognize and be aware of my old, compulsive behaviors and back away from them, moving against the fear, the anxiety, and whatever else I was dealing with and trust, trust, trust."

Betty would sit out in the middle of those warm, beautiful woods and ponder all that God was teaching her through her prayer and Bible study. One story particularly spoke to her about how Jesus handled the chaos in His own life. When the disciples found themselves in a raging storm on the Sea of Galilee, Jesus was asleep in the back of the boat. They were so frightened that they decided they had better wake Him up. He woke up and said to them, "What are you afraid of? I'm in the boat with you." Then He stilled the storm (from Luke 8:22-25). As she pondered that story, she thought to herself that if God could speak order into all of creation, then certainly God could speak order into the chaos of her life. If she could completely abandon herself into the hands of God and gradually open to receive the Love and Light that illumines the darkness and calms the storm, perhaps she could find the Still-Point within herself and become the still-point for others. This was the great hope she clung to.

The chaos around us never changes. What changes is that we begin to view the world and ourselves differently. When we are finally able to live from a place of hope moment by moment, we don't see the chaos as frightening anymore—it becomes an opportunity to offer love, presence, and compassion in the midst of it. God is all and in all, and if we are to live in Him, we must be willing to be in all too—even if that means staying in the midst of the storm. Jesus says we have a new commandment: to love one another. He is saying, "I have shown you how to love; now take it out into the chaos of the world and feed My sheep with it."

> *I made a covenant to walk with Him*
> *Where shadows fleck on mountain heights*
> *Where death steals faith and hope despairs*
> *Love whispers, calls my name,*
> *"Make of yourself a light."*

I made two copies for my returning
One I carry, ready to unroll
One I posted on heaven's gates
Deep inside my soul.

All of this inner work was gradually bringing Betty to a clearer knowing of her true self as well as enabling the presence and love of God to transform her. She was trying to step outside of herself and dispassionately observe and identify her negative behaviors and thoughts in order to separate her false self from her true one, her illusions from what was real. As she continued to do this, she became increasingly attentive to God and, at the same time, more aware of what was going on within and around her. She was seeing everything with new eyes. The line between the sacred and the secular was slowly disappearing. Everything in her life that was happening was exactly what was supposed to be happening and it was all opportunity for her healing. She was beginning to see things as they really were, not as she hoped they would be or as her biases and judgments had always seen them.

This process of observing and identifying what was happening within her is what she calls "Name, Claim, and Tame." When she became aware of a negative thought, feeling, or behavior, she named it by objectively calling it what it was, for instance, her obsessive need for privacy. Then she claimed it as part of her false self. To tame it, she simply offered it to the Holy Spirit, trusting Him to redeem it. She knew she could not transform herself, but in time and with practice, she could create the space for God to do the work of her redemption.

"I had to wake up and name the fear that was keeping me back in my little hole. My excessive need for privacy was all my stuff; it wasn't Bryant's or anybody else's. My need was not a bad thing in itself; it had just gotten way out of balance causing me to waste precious energy defending my space. God eventually redeemed that need, and it became the gift of solitude that led me to a deep understanding of so many of God's truths. My sin and my gift were two sides of the same coin, but if I hadn't done the work of taming my gift, I know it would have destroyed me.

"Energy is one of the most precious gifts God has given us, and we don't want to waste it by being drawn into negativity. All of our energy should be used for reconciliation. We always have a choice. We can either expend natural, constructive energy that comes from an intentional focus on Christ, a willing attitude, creative work, and regular exercise, or we can expend negative energy, which comes from self-pity, bitterness, and resentment. When we are living on natural energy, we will get tired but we won't burn out. That kind of energy is easily replenished by rest and exercise. There is another form of energy that arises with fear. The adrenaline created is meant to be used strictly for crisis situations, so if we constantly run on that energy, we will find ourselves depleted and exhausted. Either energy can be used within the circumstances God has placed us, but one will lead to life and renewed energy and the other will lead to death and burnout."

She redirected her negative energy by quietly stepping back into the gentle, transforming silence of attentiveness, paying attention to what she was feeling and surrendering those feelings to God. This involved a calm willingness to wait and watch for God to work in the situation, but it was followed by a much clearer discernment of what, if any, action she needed to take. She was learning to be inspired rather than impulsive. If she hadn't done this work, her compulsions would have remained alive in her and she would have continued to waste valuable energy that God wanted her to use for love and healing.

"The ultimate end of all of this is: How better can we love? Learning to love takes time and endless practice. Life will always be offering us challenges to convert our negative perceptions into loving ones, but given time and patience and a quiet place of Presence, we will come to know a new way. Love bends. It doesn't demand its rights; it's free like the sea foam that skims across the incoming tide. If we choose to open ourselves to God's mercy, the Spirit of Love will transform us because we are clearing our inner selves of self and moving more and more into His likeness."

Illumination

Trust and letting go work mysteriously together. Nothing ever stays the same in our lives, and again and again we are called to let go in order to find a new way. If we continue to cling to the past and never dare to let go, we will never learn to trust. If we never trust, we will never dare to let go. Our choice is this: to become more bound up trying to fight the reality we find ourselves in and hold on to our illusion of control, or to become more free by trusting God's goodness and desire to move us to a new place of freedom. The more we believe that God truly loves us and wants what is best for us, the easier it becomes to believe that everything that is happening is exactly as it should be.

The first step is submission—surrender to God. We have to let go of how we perceive that things and people in our life should be, take off our god-coats and let God be God. As we do this, we are slowly making the shift from temporal values to eternal values. The second step is to allow some time for God to work and for circumstances to unfold, enabling us to see things a little clearer before we act. We tend to be impulsive, but we need to learn to listen and wait for the inspiration of the Holy Spirit. "You tell me what to do, Lord. You tell me when to move." The third step is to accept in love and trust whatever happens, however it happens, whenever it happens. That doesn't mean it will not be painful, but this silent acceptance of however He chooses to enter our life will soften us and enable us to move into a place of healing despite the pain. Finally, as Jesus exhorts us, once we put our hand to the plow, we are not to look back, trusting that seeds of new life are being planted that will unfold into something far more beautiful than anything our finite minds could ever grasp or hope for. "No eye has seen, no ear has heard, no mind has conceived what God has prepared for those who love him (1 Corinthians 2:9)."

This kind of detaching and letting go demands a tremendous amount of solitude, silence, and prayer. We cannot do it otherwise, because the pressure to conform is so great. If we will persevere, though, we will discover that underneath the outer life we live is another life—a hidden, inner life in Christ. When we find this ground of our being and learn to live from this place, we will finally become the still-point, the reconciling factor, in the midst of the chaos in our families, our work, and our world.

I pray always that these words may awaken in you more of His Spirit and help you to unravel more of His secrets.

Betty

Beloved — where, when
Will this painful grieving end
This joyful, sorrowful
Returning to what has been?
Memories revisited in my solitude
Memories revisited in deepest gratitude.

In a thousand things
I've seen the beauty of Your Face
My heart bent, broken by Your Grace.

Around a thousand corners
I've glimpsed Your Shadow
Still and silent gazed
Then felt Your Loving Presence fade.

In a thousand nights and days
I've heard the whisper of Your Voice
Submitted, yielded to Your Way.

Yet now amid the turbulence of pain, of change
I feel assurance often slip away
And come to know once more
In a thousand hidden ways
That trust is known in steadfast Faith
That healing Light is found in Hope
That all of Life is held in Love.

BWS

CHAPTER TWELVE

UNFOLDING

BEAUTY

Creation was helping Betty do this work of naming, claiming, and taming and detaching from her false self. The more she walked in the quiet beauty at The Old Still, the more free she became from the fear, the old voices, and the demands of the culture or "the tribe" as she calls it. Solitude was helping to empty her of all this. Her relationship with God was becoming so real and intimate that she was feeling less need to look anywhere else for love and affirmation.

She faithfully followed the spiritual discipline of having her quiet time in the morning and the physical discipline of walking or running every day. On her walks, she meditated on a verse she had read in Scripture during her devotional time and tried to hear what God might be saying to her through His creation. As she did this, her eyes began to open to a far deeper beauty.

"On my walks I talked to God the whole time. These were extended periods of quiet that were waking me up. The solitude, silence, and contemplative walking were really my antidepressants. When things were stressful, I became consciously aware of my inclination toward self-pity and repeated a phrase from Scripture over and over, asking the Holy Spirit to change my perception, to take my focus from myself and turn to God. These holy words are beyond what we can comprehend, beyond our finite minds, and were counteracting the voices of my false-self system. I made a choice to open up more of myself to God, and in that choice, the healing love of God began to pour in. My feelings followed my choices. I was just overwhelmed with the beauty of the dogwoods and the flush of the trees as the sunlight flashed through the lime green leaves of spring. I was seeing for the first time.

"I was beginning to tie everything that I was seeing in nature to what I was learning in Scripture. I watched how the osprey frantically defended their nests. Their squawk actually sounded like they were screaming at me, 'Stay back, this is mine, mine, mine!' The little wiry-headed foxes followed me suspiciously with their dark eyes, intently watching from their holes when I came too close. It all made me think of the Scripture that says the birds and foxes have their nests, but the Son of Man has no place to lay His head. In the past, I thought that was an external thing—you know, 'Poor Jesus, He didn't have a house, He just roamed around preaching.' Now, I began to think that God was saying to me that I wasn't to claim anything for myself. I have a bed, but it is not mine. My attitude needed to be one of letting go and gratitude. 'The Lord gives and the Lord takes away. Thank you, Lord, for what You have given me today.'

"It seemed to me, as I gazed at the sunlight glistening off the heavy dew on the spiderwebs that I call 'wood webs,' that their very weight made them beautiful, so perhaps the weight I was carrying and the depression I had been struggling with and the mysteries I still didn't understand could become a thing of beauty too. What was interesting to me was that, without the additional weight of the dew, I don't think the beauty would have been there. It spoke to me of my inner journey, of walking in the light of Christ's love and allowing that light to create something beautiful from the weight of my suffering. This was a tremendous encouragement, and it was all revealed to me in the simplicity of the morning dew.

"In creation, God offered me a gift that was not at all threatening. Being a fearful person, I needed to bring something inside myself that was beyond me and was not frightening. Love was manifesting Himself to me through creation and it was stilling my fear. I know now that as I brought God's perfect love into me, it cast out all of my fear and healed me."

Against the gray ground fog of morning
the wood webs sag under heavy drops of dew.
Yet as the sun breaks through
the moisture turns to silver.
Endless weight becomes a thing of beauty.

"One way to bring God into ourselves is to discover Him outside of ourselves. I found Him in creation, but others might find Him in the love of another, a painting, or a magnificent piece of music. These are hints of Something beyond us and far greater than us. We have been given this capacity to transcend ourselves. We hear the Voice within calling us His beloved and we know, just for that moment in time, that there is something way beyond calling us home to our true self, calling us home to the Christ-self that has been put in us from the beginning of time. Opening ourselves to receive Him by savoring these moments of heightened perception brings us into a deeper and deeper oneness and love relationship with God. Now when we say to someone the words, 'I love you,' those words can change a life because it is not us saying them any longer; it is the Beloved, the Holy One, the One who has chosen us to speak His love to others. Creation taught me this. I was seeing God's love in everything and allowing it to fill me. I didn't say anything to anyone about all of this for many years; I just tried to quietly press it into my heart."

Let me seek again
This place of solitude and silence,
This inner poverty,
This space that claims nothing for itself.
Where everything I touch is prayer
For God is there.

The house was coming along, and Betty and Bryant were both enjoying the process immensely. Bryant was doing most of the architectural planning, and Betty was doing the interior design. When it was finished, they had a warm, inviting home that faded quietly into the landscape. It was so quiet that often, when Bryant came into the living room to build a fire in the huge brick fireplace in the early mornings, he would find deer from the surrounding woods sleeping outside the screen door.

"I loved to garden and I could lose myself talking to my plants, nurturing them, and watching them grow. It was in my garden that I began to get a sense of the flow of the giving and receiving of love because every morning it offered me so much beauty in return for my care. I worked with the wild deer that lived on the property and received so much back from them too. I was especially attached to Bama, my pet deer. He was a sweet little buck whose mother had been killed, so I adopted him. Bama followed me all over the place. When he and Babe had triplets, I named them Tom, Dick, and Harry. It takes an awful lot of patience to work with wildlife, because you have to watch their behavior very carefully. All of this was refining the observer in me."

The Old Still was a wonderful place for entertaining and Bryant was always having huge parties there. He didn't think it was a party if there weren't at least 250 people coming, so Betty had her work cut out for her. She had to maintain the place and have everything ready whenever he decided to bring a crowd in. When the kids brought their friends home from college for the annual Georgia-Florida football game, she would set the boys up in sleeping bags in the trailer and the girls would stay in the house. Bryant lit a huge bonfire out in the woods, and on Sunday Betty would fix a beautiful southern brunch for them with vegetables and fresh-cut flowers from her garden. Georgia-Florida at The Old Still got to be a hot ticket at the University of Florida.

Betty was having a wonderful time, but underneath it all she had the same deep longing for solitude. Rather than letting that tension defeat her again, though, she determinedly kept her balance and focus through her daily spiritual and physical disciplines. Her energy was increasing because she wasn't wasting it by allowing herself to get tangled up in old fears or by being drawn into and overwhelmed by Bryant's strong energy.

"I was no longer listening to those old voices and was trying to listen to the Holy Spirit, but to do that, I needed to have my quiet time every morning and then get outside and walk. I had a lot of responsibilities because Bryant was still very involved in the community and was forever hosting huge events at The Old Still that I had to put together. In the past, I would have resented the intrusion of so many people, but I began to understand that these were not just Bryant's people—they were my people too, because God loved them. All people are God's people and I simply had to welcome them in love. I was seeing that the heart of God and the heart of the suffering world are the same.

"These were simple truths that were moving me toward wholeness. I was getting more and more deeply in touch with the fact that gratitude is everything. I had always tended to look for what was missing in my life and overlooked what was there. Only in gratitude could I return something to God. And what did He want me to return? A re-created self, an integrated, whole person. I understood this and was standing at last on solid ground, in the now that never passes away."

Help me to remember, Father,
that this time of joy

will never come again.
Let me savor the fullness of it.
Let me share the beauty of it
that others might feel
and know it too.

"During this time, I was given the opportunity to hike in the Swiss Alps. It was there that I woke up to the reality of the gift of preparation and the necessity of perseverance. I had persevered with my exercise regimen, so I was now physically very strong and able to make the trip. I was seeing with new eyes, so I was prepared to recognize what was to be a great turning point in my life. That day, the alpine sky was shrouded in clouds, and I had been walking for several hours. I was feeling so good physically, breathing the crisp, clear, alpine air and the wondrous scent of the meadow filled with wildflowers. I was connecting with everything around me with a depth of awareness that I had never felt before. It was almost noon, so I stopped to eat a little lunch. As I was lying there in the meadow, feeling the cool breeze play across my eyelids, I felt a deep sense of Presence and an ecstasy of belonging that I had never before experienced. When I opened my eyes, the mist had lifted and the clouds suddenly parted, unveiling the most magnificent sight I had ever seen: the Matterhorn. Its great, craggy, granite peak rose out of the ink blue sky like a monstrous cathedral spire blanketed in ghostly snow. It seemed that it was looming over only me, highlighting the beauty and the mystery and the wonder of God. In that moment, I experienced a sweet, unmistakable sense that God knew my suffering and was affirming and encouraging me to persevere. I had a deep sense that if God would show me such beauty, then He would surely have even more out there for me. So now, etched in my mind and heart, there was no longer a question of my commitment to the cost or the discipline involved in the journey; I was going to persevere. And I did. And I have. And I still do. My experience on the Matterhorn that day was truly prayer because it moved me toward God in a powerful way. Any movement toward God is prayer. Perseverance now became a way of life, a way to Life eternal."

There is no Amen in prayer
for those who seek and find
it is always there.

All of her suffering had prepared Betty for this moment in time. Because she had disciplined herself to get out of bed and walk, she could walk in the mountains. Because she walked, she learned to see with new eyes. Because she saw with new eyes, she was able to receive the gift of that day. Because she received the gift of that day, she knew there would be more. Everything is preparation; nothing is wasted. When the work of our preparation, process, and perseverance begins to merge, we gradually become aware of the breathtaking reality of the Holy One in the depths of our soul and in all of creation.

She was still in process, but as she submitted to the leadings of the Spirit of Love, trusting Him enough to actually try to live out what He asked of her each day, she became more alive and began to participate in life in a deeper, more loving way—Christ's way. By returning again and again to the Source in this contemplative and reflective posture, she moved from her head into her heart that had been softened by Love and found to her amazement that she was becoming a reconciler, a healer in her wounded world. This required a great deal of humility and obscurity but she didn't count the cost and she no longer looked for anything in return. The wonderful gift in it was that, the more she found the courage to offer the love she was experiencing to others, the more love was returned to her and the more her journey accelerated.

God was preparing Betty to experience this deeper love by giving her the time in creation she had always yearned for. She was now confident and comfortable enough in her hiking skills to be alone in the mountains.

While hiking in Switzerland, she had met a German woman who taught her the rudiments of mountain walking. Annie, a survivor of the Holocaust, emphasized to her the importance of having very good boots, socks, and rain gear. A whistle and compass were critical in case she got lost, as well as plenty of water and a simple healthy lunch. She taught Betty to set a breathing pattern of inhaling and exhaling that flowed with her steps, and to set her own pace and stride and stay with it. The European way of mountain walking (Annie never called it hiking) is not to compete to get there first but to reach your goal sometime during the day without being burned out, knowing that the joy and the goal is the journey itself.

Betty took these skills back with her to the mountains of North Carolina where she and Bryant had been spending the summer for the last few years. As she walked there more and more, she got very good at reading her compass and developed a keen sense of direction that allowed her to get off the beaten path to find hidden, quiet places. These were the places where God would sweetly reveal to her the depths of the hidden life and her true self.

It's His great, broad, free land
  that surrounds me.
It's His forest where silence
  has lease.
It's His mountain where stillness
  Abounds.
It's His beauty that fills me
  with wonder.
It's His soft, gentle voice that
  impels me.
It's His Presence that fills me
  with peace.

Illumination

If we are going to hear the inner Voice of Love speaking to us in very soft and gentle ways, it is imperative that we take time to be alone in a quiet place and embrace the silence. Silence teaches us to listen. The Voice of Love is speaking to us all the time, but the noise of the world, with its loud distractions and false voices, is very, very difficult to turn off. Our task on the journey inward is to learn to listen for this Voice, immerse ourselves in its Love, wrap ourselves up in the silence, and open our hearts to the Spirit of God.

Silence is God's language and it gently draws us to our depths. We are drawn into the Word that gives life and power to all of our spoken words. Silence changes our understanding of Scripture because our illusions and false voices are no longer clouding it. Truth comes alive in us and we begin to discern with clarity, purity, and depth how God is interpreting Scripture to us. Silence guards and nourishes the truth within our hearts. If we immediately go out and speak about such holy things, we lose their transforming power because we haven't allowed time for the Spirit to press them into our hearts. Our words dilute their strength.

This transforming silence involves a deliberate choice to withdraw into solitude. There is a difference between solitude and loneliness. When we are lonely, we can't come to silence because, subconsciously, the false self is trying to figure out ways of not being lonely. The endless monologue of the ego is constantly interpreting reality in a way that keeps us bound up in grasping, fear. Solitude can be a painful place at first because we haven't yet learned to turn our minds off and listen for the Beloved in silence. Our mind constantly tells us there are things to be done, that we are wasting time, and that we are doing a poor job of having a quiet time. We haven't yet come to a sense of abiding in God, the sweet and holy oneness of friendship with God. It takes a tremendous amount of discipline at first, but if we will come and endeavor to be silent, to be still and to listen, it gets easier. The more we come to the silence, the more we hear, and the more we hear, the more we come to the silence.

Treasuring every moment, pressing it all in, nourished by hunger,

Betty

Present in the moment,
At one with Thee,
In a mountain meadow
Created just for me.
Backed against a rough barked tree
Resting . . . just resting.
A rest so deep, so sweet,
As to be asleep to temporal things.

To see the clouds as hinged to heaven,
And opened now and then,
To let Your voice,
The echo of the wind, pass through.
It's You, my Beloved,
Calling me to life.

To feel the movement
Of the branches that dance,
Caught in the currents of Your breath,
Unseen, yes, but there.
It's You, my Beloved,
Touching me to life.

To see the shadows as Your hand,
Covering the valley far below,
The sunlight glistening between
Your gentle fingers.
It's You, my Beloved,
Warming cold hearts to life.

To know You, my Beloved,
As Creation speaks,
Is to know that Life Eternal
Comes from temporal sleep.

BWS

CHAPTER THIRTEEN

LIGHT THROUGH
BROKEN GLASS

The eighties were years that moved Betty into uncharted inner as well as outer terrain, opening her more and more to her hidden self. This opening was born out of conscious choices, acts of love, and relentless seeking, profoundly deepening her experience of God and her relationships with others.

The recovery period of her life had come to an end now. On one level, her life with Bryant was fun and very full. They went fishing and bird hunting, watched their children get married, cheered on the Gators, and continued to host parties and political rallies at The Old Still as well as in North Carolina. Though she was no longer on the team, she was still so good at tennis that people would come to her for lessons at what they called her Training Camp in the Deep Woods. Beneath this active pace, however, the Spirit of God was at work, tilling the inner landscape of her heart, preparing her for an even deeper intimacy and sense of oneness with Him and His creation. There was never a day in all of her recovery work and all of her activity with Bryant that she did not ponder the possibility of a deeper plan that God might have for her life.

In 1980, her daughter-in-law called and asked her to join Bible Study Fellowship (BSF), an intensive Bible study they were trying to bring to Jacksonville. They needed to sign up sixty people in advance so they could get the materials to get started. It was as if the Holy Spirit was saying to her, "Okay, Betty, it's time to make another change." She signed up and was asked to be a small-group leader. Everything in her wanted to say yes, but God said no. "Betty, all I want you to do is take your mother to the Bible study. That's your work right now."

"I had worked very hard throughout the seventies to reestablish my relationships with my husband and children, but there was one relationship left that was not healed—my relationship with my mother. I was finally mature enough in my spirituality to understand that she was never going to change and I needed to accept that and meet her where she was in love. The people closest to us can hurt us so deeply that their wounding forever marks us, making it very difficult to forgive them, and I had struggled to forgive my mother. When I was at last emptied enough of the resentment and judgmental attitude I had held onto for so long, I was able to see the Light, the face of Christ, shining in the broken glass that was my mother. She had deeply wounded me, but it was only because she had been wounded. She didn't do it intentionally; it was just all she knew. When I truly began to see her that way, she began to feel my love rather than my resentment and our relationship healed."

> *In believing, my old cup is broken,*
> *In forgiveness, my broken cup becomes whole,*
> *In love, my new cup is made clean,*
> *In seeking, my cup is refilled,*
> *In thanksgiving, my cup runneth over.*

"I made a very conscious choice to commit my time to my mother and simply be there for her. I knew this would be very costly for me because she would ask me to do things with her that I didn't like to do at all. Nevertheless, I called her and told her that, if she would go with me to BSF on Wednesday mornings, we would spend the afternoons together doing whatever she would like to do. I had no expectations. I didn't know how she would respond when I called. I just trusted God with it. She was thrilled to death with the idea because, until then, I had been very distant from her, not only in miles but also in my heart. Healing love is sacrificial and if I had not been willing to take the initiative and go the second mile, forgiveness and reconciliation would have been very difficult to attain."

It had taken a long time for Betty to get to the place where she could forgive her mother, but her long road to recovery had taught her that waiting is one of the most difficult yet integral pieces in our spiritual journey. We have to allow God time to work in our life and in the lives of others. Most often, that takes far longer than we think it should. So Betty forgave Annie Tartt and waited. She followed through with her commitment and every Wednesday morning at 8:00 she drove across town to pick her up. They would arrive at the church at 9:00 and sit in the place Annie Tartt had chosen on the left side, second row from the front, same seat every Wednesday, year in and year out, for the next seven years. If they arrived and anyone happened to be sitting in her seat, Annie Tartt would make them move. That was her seat and that was just the way it was. After Bible study, they went to lunch at the club and spent the rest of the afternoon shopping or doing anything else Annie Tartt wanted to do.

"I am called by Love to lay down my life and go the second mile in love. How I choose to live my life, moment by moment, is either going to help bring the world together in Christ or to separate it. God engineers my circumstances. It is how I respond to them that makes the difference. I can't change or fix anything, but I can live in the circumstances as a whole person and offer love in the midst of it all.

"It is all heart attitude. My opinions, my biases, and my prejudices are not the whole picture. I can learn to keep my mouth closed and my heart open when a conflict arises. Now, I try to simply be quietly present to the other person in love, absorbing any painful arrows of negativity as our Lord did. It is important to understand that when I do this, I am not being a doormat. A doormat is motivated by fear rather than love and has no divine purpose in mind. I still speak my truth when I feel called to, but I try to only do it when I am focused and able to speak it in love.

"Love that freely offers forgiveness and genuine forgiveness draws us into communion. It flows from a heart that is free. It is the name of love in a wounded world. The only way I can become free enough within myself to forgive those who have wounded me is to make a conscious choice to release them. This releasing grows from a sorrowful and compassionate awareness of the frailties and failings of every human heart. For example, I could finally look at Mama and see her brokenness rather than her failure to give me what I needed. If I had continued to blame her, define her, defend myself, or deny my own brokenness, how could God ever set me free from all the knots of that painful and twisted relationship? None of this had anything to do with her. It really only had to do with me, my journey, and how I could change. So instead of focusing on all of the negative things about her, I chose to look at the positive. By doing that, I was releasing her.

"I had been wasting so much energy in 'if only' and 'why me?' Self-pity is a false-self trap and I had to consciously push against it. Coming to God in quiet to try to change my focus enabled me to receive the love so I could then go out and offer it to my mother. Slowly, my heart attitude moved from one of resentment to one of gratitude. I couldn't bring back the lost years, but as I learned to keep my focus, reconnect to the Source, and gently allow myself time to grow, I knew I could offer an awful lot in the years I had left. When we are judging or condemning, we are incapable of actively engaging in intercession. We are called to love unconditionally from a pure heart. Only then can we lift others to Him, Who is forgiveness. This movement of healing love reflects, in a finite way, both the manner in which God forgives us and the costliness of His infinitely precious gift. So we make the offering of forgiveness, we trust God, and we wait in faith and hope for the mystery to unravel."

When Betty finally got back to The Old Still late in the afternoon, and if God cleared the way, she would spend some time walking in the woods or doing her Bible study lesson for the next week back in what she called her "little quiet room." Her commitment to the work of reconciliation within her family and the disciplines she had learned in her recovery were now part of the fabric of how she lived her life. All of this was feeding her soul and all of it was done very quietly. She had learned how important it was for her to press in—or ponder quietly in her heart—those things that God was revealing to her. The Beloved was offering her these intimate glimpses of truth, and she wanted to be present to it all with quality, holding them and pondering them in the hidden sanctuary of her soul. She had already acquired extensive head knowledge of the Scriptures and the great spiritual writings but this quiet pressing in was bringing it all down into her heart.

Dear friend, on the path coming home.
Press in, press in, oh press in
Your ear ever close to the Source.
You will hear, though you still may be sleeping
His voice gently awakening within.
You will know with a knowing beyond knowing

How Love's Spirit weaves the ways of your days,
How Love's fire kindles the twigs of desire,
How Love's longing becomes your belonging.

In her morning quiet times, she would ask God what He wanted her to take with her on her walk that day. There were many mornings that she took just one little line from Scripture or from spiritual writers that were speaking to her like Oswald Chambers or Amy Carmichael. Often, she would spend an entire summer in one book and she might meditate on one phrase from a book or Scripture for several days. She would read very slowly, pausing between words, engaging her senses and imagination as she pondered and opened to what God was saying to her through the writings of these holy men and women. What she was actually doing is the time-honored spiritual discipline of *lectio divina*: meditative reading. For her, it was much more than a method for gaining knowledge; it was a rich source of nourishment and holy joy for her soul and a habit of the heart that led her to an intimate experience of the presence of God. Oddly enough, on every step of her journey, Betty experienced a truth or was led to a spiritual practice, such as lectio divina, before she had a name for it. Later, she would read about it in one of her books and realize that was what she had been experiencing.

She didn't have a spiritual director, because Bryant had never allowed her to attend Christian retreats or seminars. God was her teacher and continued to give her spiritual friends and mentors through books. She was still careful to keep her reading in balance with the rest of her life. The great evangelical writers of the nineteenth and twentieth centuries, such as Hudson Taylor, Dwight L. Moody, Andrew Murray, and A. W. Tozer were the people God sent at that time to feed her hunger for a deeper walk with Christ. Amy Carmichael's simplicity, absolute surrender to God, and courageous defiance of the missionary structure and Tozer's habit of getting up every morning at 5:00 to pray on the banks of Lake Michigan, even in the bitterest Chicago weather, spoke powerfully to her. Hudson Taylor's practice of getting up at 4:00 a.m. to light a candle and meditate impacted her commitment to the practice of prayer. Their lives of trust and obedience inspired her and prepared her for the deeper places God was taking her.

"These contemplative walks at The Old Still were awakening me to the minute details of creation. I walked slowly, talking to God, observing and listening to every sound in the woods. I was developing a very keen awareness of my senses. I wanted to touch and feel and sense everything He created and let it speak back to me about His love. The more we hear, see, touch, smell, and feel of God, the more we have of Him; and the more we have of Him, the more of Him we can give away. Every little leaf, every little shadow, every little spiderweb was speaking to me about God, and I would come in and endeavor to write in my journal the thought or the lesson that the Holy Spirit was bringing to my attention. The little writings were not well articulated, but I kept trying and they got a little better. I kept trying because those who encouraged me, the great spiritual writers, had kept trying.

"Three important things were happening in my spiritual journey then and later in the mountain years: I was detaching more from the world in a healthy way, I was reading Scripture in a totally new way through attentive listening and meditation, and I was doing the final work of reconciliation with my mother. I was living the contemplative life but I had no idea it had a name. The three pieces were coming together and they were feeding each other. I didn't set it up at all. God did it; I was just obedient to it. In this way, I began to rediscover the 'I Am' in the depths of my soul. He had been there all the time, but I had to wake up to the reality of Him.

"This movement toward God required that I become a partaker of solitude, silence, and prayer, and He graciously gave me ten years of that. I know very few people have the gift of time that I had, but as I reflect on that I don't think it is the quantity of time as much as the quality of our heart's desire to be with Him. If we will cultivate this intensity of desire, God will make a way.

"This was my work but every journey is unique. Each seeking heart is touched in a special way, marked by its own re-created beauty and relationship with the Holy One. My work was the coming and allowing

Jesus to embrace me, to change me, to free me to be who He had created me to be and to learn those disciplines and practices that would make me more conscious of His presence. Ultimately, the spiritual work for all of us is to take our identity from the One who calls us His beloved. God was paving the way for me to experience these truths in a transformational way."

> O Christ, I cannot hold Thee close enough.
> Again and again I come
> To gaze into the beauty
>   of Your dark, compelling eyes,
> To feel the wonder
>   of Your passion and Your sighs,
> To touch the edges,
>   the mystery of Your love.
> O Christ, I cannot hold Thee close enough.

Illumination

Jesus says, "I tell you the truth, whatever you bind on earth will be bound in heaven, and whatever you loose on earth will be loosed in heaven" (Matthew 18:18). This beautiful Scripture speaks to how God honors our choices, particularly those that are in the direction of reconciliation, healing, and love. God will not force us to choose to forgive, but if we do not, He will not be able to set us free from the broken relationships that keep us bound up in fear, anger, and shame.

Reconciliation requires that we release people from our anger and resentment. We cannot come to the altar in conflict. If we aren't moving in the direction of being reconciled to others, how can we be reconciled to God? We choose our own binding. If we don't choose to be free, we will never be free.

We are beloved of God. God has already forgiven us, so we don't have to be down on ourselves anymore, but we do have to come to prayer in repentance to receive the love. The work of reconciliation is to get in touch with the fact that the love we have received enables us to take the initiative to go out and offer it. Love always takes the initiative to reach back in forgiveness to the one who wounded us. If we are to blame for a negative situation, without the empowering of genuine love, we are not going to be able to go vulnerably and openly to ask for forgiveness and have it mean anything because we will take it right back in our next action. Once we truly believe that God has released us, we don't feel resentment and anger anymore and His love enables us to truly release another. The relationship then becomes sweeter because the love we have received has been poured out in the midst of the turmoil.

Jesus places no limits on His forgiving love. He takes the mud and the silt of our common humanity and transforms it, changes it by grace, resting all on the foundation stone of forgiveness. Might we open our hearts ever wider to receive Christ's love in rebuilding our own lives on the foundation stone of forgiveness.

In His love that holds the whole of humanity in a compassionate embrace,

Betty

Trapped in flesh's solitude,
my spirit
weary, worn, forlorn
from decades of relentless seeking
for that one Door
through which all the fires go
until only embers glow;
that sacred Center
where no one else can enter,
where all the many things are One.

Morning slowly comes to consciousness,
my prayers
stretched tight across the silent sky
awakened by the beauty of the golden dawn
shake free the endless circles
of a dark and fearful night.
The senses fuse sight, touch and sound are one
and all to splendor run,
rise high on blazing diamonds of a pure and selfless love
up to a sunlit day.

Emptied of all denial and deceit,
my poverty
absolute at last complete,
quietly into His epiphany I walk
toward light seen in music that was never heard
and softness spoken that was not a word.
Oh, the love, the wonder in the blazing diamonds gaze!
And I?
I must arise in faith and go
by inward passage from what earth I know.

BWS

CHAPTER FOURTEEN

THE

COLOR OF CHANGE

The beauty and the silence of the mountains were drawing Betty more and more. Bryant loved the summers in North Carolina too, so they decided to build a house there. He bought a beautiful wooded lot in a growing resort community and designed a huge home with a separate guesthouse, but the project didn't get off the ground before the trouble began. The septic tank ran over, the costs ran up, and the contractor ran off. Betty had always wanted something much simpler, so she suggested they look at a little spec house she had seen in a quiet, isolated development farther up the mountain. They went there, peeked in the windows, liked what they saw, and decided to buy it. The developer was a friend, so Bryant called him that night with an offer. It was accepted, the papers were drawn up the next day, and the house was theirs.

Betty created a quiet, simple living space using soothing, muted colors from nature and a few of the antiques they had collected over the years. The house was situated on the north face of Rock Mountain. Laurel Knob and Cow Rock loomed weightlessly in the distance beyond the scarlet red geraniums blooming on the deck. Sitting out there, it was so quiet she could almost hear the air. Its coolness had a clarity that excited her senses and grounded her soul. She loved that little house, and she had a sense that God would use it in a special way she did not yet see.

"One day, after a long mountain walk, I came in and threw myself down on the sofa to rest, and the Spirit of God just washed over me to the point that it brought tears to my eyes. It was as if God was saying to me, 'Betty, this little house is being sanctified by Me and it will be used to glorify Me.'"

She had seen the fall color change in the Blue Ridge Mountains many times in the past, but now she was seeing it all differently. She was experiencing God in a new and far deeper way in the beauty of creation and nature's changing palette, and this vision was profoundly impacting her.

"I remember one October in particular. The color change was the most spectacular one I had ever seen and I was excited to death to get out in it. Looking back, I wonder whether it was really that beautiful or whether I was just seeing it with new eyes. There is a tremendous difference between looking and seeing. When you're looking, you're in your head and you're not attuned to the Spirit of God. I didn't want to look anymore. I wanted to see the color, feel the color, and experience God in it. I wanted to be with God, immersed and wrapped in His love."

> Now, again, I behold
> Landscape reaching up to touch the sky
> Through wreaths of multicolored leaves
> Floating and spinning among the trees.
> Brilliant blue against the gold,
> Autumn, the season of my soul.

"One morning I got up early to walk up the mountain. It was a bright, sunny day and I don't think there is anything more beautiful than the early morning sunlight highlighting a color change. It is so exquisite it makes you cry. I walked and walked and walked and filled up and filled up and filled up, but I just couldn't get enough of the warm feeling of God's presence. So when evening came, I went to a place where the sun sets and closed my day with God, looking out over the glorious painting of creation that He had made and makes new every fall. I was experiencing more and more a profound sense of oneness and I knew that God was walking with me. I was beginning to understand that God's love encompasses all of creation and all of humanity because He creates, loves, and sustains it all. I was waking up to the wonder and beauty of God in a deep, deep interior place. God, for me, was coming out of the box I had put Him in with my opinions, fears, and cultural conditioning and was speaking to me through the magnificence of that spectacular color change."

Oh, Love,
If such beauty extinguish me,
If I gain Your Spirit free,
If death, its agony, its ecstasy
bloom my eternity;
It's then I'll know I've nothing left to bring.
For sun just touched the morning
and all my life is Spring.
Moment by moment, Beloved, I'm Yours.

"I know it is hard to imagine having either the time or the patience to spend a whole day in God's presence but, if our desire for Him is intense enough, we will find the time and God will honor our choices with His presence. He sweetly gave me His Spirit that day in the color change. I was not aware of myself, only the warmth of God's presence with me. I was totally free in that moment in time, lost in awe and amazement. The love of God was enveloping me and I didn't want it to end. He led me home, back to the garden where there is no awareness of self, only a deep sense of oneness with Him and His beautiful creation. Perhaps that's what that color change was for me that day—a day in the Garden of Eden. These moments are eternal and they will live in my heart forever."

> *O Love, struggling to break through.*
> *Why am I so blind to simple things?*
> *The hush of Your Presence that the meadow brings*
> *Are but fragments of infinite loving, never my own.*
> *The depth of Your secrets are still hidden from view*
> *Way beyond mountains, meadows and skies.*
> *Please, Love, embrace me; open my eyes.*
> *Burn in me brightly. Light the whole world.*

Even though she was taking a lot of time to walk alone on the mountain, Betty was still very involved in the social life of Cashiers, North Carolina. She was hosting Bryant's golf events, going to dinner parties, and traveling back to Florida every weekend in the fall to watch her Gators play. But when God cleared some time for her, she packed her rucksack and went up the mountain to be alone with Him. She was deepening her capacity to be present in and enjoy the moments God gave her. Her first Love was calling, and the more she responded, the clearer that love-cry became.

"God led me to the mountains to remember. 'Try to remember, Betty, whose and who you are. You belong to Me, and this is how I created you.' Getting in touch with silence and solitude and gradually letting go of some of the social activities that were taking my time and energy is really what was happening. I knew that I had to decide to either detach or not detach from all of that. My friends and family didn't understand what I was doing, and I began to get comments about being a loner and a hermit and comments like, 'You come up here and you don't even let us know you're here.' But if everybody knew I was there, the phone would start ringing, and all of the 'Why haven't you called and how about supper tonight?'

would start. That didn't mean I was not going to do those things. I knew better than to get out of balance again. I just did them when Bryant was there. I wanted very much to go to the mountain and be alone with God, but I was learning that I wasn't to claim anything or have any expectations. I was just to do what needed to be done and trust God for a little quiet time with Him later. So when God cleared the way, I went up the mountain. The more I did that, the deeper the time became, and the more the sacred mysteries began to unravel. It takes time—quiet time—to reflect, and God was so faithful to give me that gift. I was making choices to be with Him and He was honoring them."

It is difficult for Jesus
to come into a life
that allows
no time for meditation
no void for contemplation.

"So many things that used to threaten me ceased to be fearful. I was no longer afraid of being drawn into and overwhelmed by Bryant's energy. I could go to parties relaxed and unself-conscious now because I went with a new desire to simply offer love. I began to trust the flow of whatever the day brought. So, when Bryant came back, the busy world of my reality came back and that was fine. Everything I had drawn into myself that God had given me in my days of solitude was now to be used and offered to others. More and more I realized it was very, very simple: it was simply Love."

Every morning she would wake up before sunrise to be with God as the new day quietly broke over Rock Mountain. She prepared for it by laying out her clothes before she went to bed so she wouldn't have to turn on a light to get dressed. She poured a cup of the hot coffee she had set up the night before and sat in her favorite chair looking out over the shrouded mountain, silently waiting for the new day. Some days were misty and sorrowful, some were clear and hopeful, some were rainy and comforting, but they were always sweet, sweet times. When the Spirit led, she prayed. As her quiet time came to a close, she read from her Bible and her dog-eared copy of *My Utmost for His Highest*. Breakfast was always simple and healthy: usually hot oat bran and raisins.

Chuckling quietly, she says, "I developed a pattern that was helping me center and focus my attention. I asked the Holy Spirit how many raisins to put in my oat bran and what each one represented as I prayed and stirred it into the bowl that, to me, was the world. It might be a prayer for someone the Spirit brought to mind or it might be a prayer asking God to unravel a mystery to me. Then I would take my tray over to my little table by the window and very, very slowly break bread with and enjoy it very much. I was trying to learn discernment, to listen to God. When I walked in the mountains, I would often pick gaylax leaves to send to a friend. They are so beautiful and they last so long that they always make me think of lingering love. I would always try to discern exactly how many to pick, and each time I put one in the little stack, I would say a prayer for that person. When the gift was received, it was a little box full of prayers. I know these sound like small things but these disciplined patterns of consciously focusing on and listening to God really impacted my life.

"It was in silence that I met God and finally awakened to who I truly was. The struggle against the compulsions of the false self and the encounter with the loving God are the essence of the search for the true self. Between these two poles, it seems, I have struggled all my life to become complete, to shed my false self and take on a new awareness, a re-created self—the Christ self. It has been an ongoing, relentless struggle between the overwhelming fears that paralyze me and the love that enlarges me beyond measure. That very struggle, though, was where my transformation took place and without my consent to it and the discipline to willingly participate in it with love and trust, I question whether I would have ever had a direct and intimate encounter with the Holy One.

"Such time alone, such meditation and contemplation, such giving and receiving, opened my heart more and more to God's voice, reminding me that in Him there is nothing but love and that I was created out of His first love for me. It is this First Love that I had to keep returning to in prayer. The returning is difficult — it is a great struggle — but if we are faithful, we will taste peace somewhere deeply hidden within our hearts, far beyond feelings and emotions. It is the peace that passes understanding. It is the God within. It will bring Christ to you and you to Him. That's what was happening to me during those years in the mountains."

In Christ the struggle transforms us.
In Christ the fire purifies us.
In Christ the pain teaches us compassion.

"In this time of solitude in creation, I was also learning to detach more and more from my old ways of thinking and attach to the Truth being revealed by the one immanent and transcendent God. I was quietly being taken beyond myself. We all desperately need to recover this sense of the Beyond in our midst in order to revive the springs of the mystery, beauty, and wonder of God. Creation is the Spirit's scaffolding. We cannot touch the Spirit, but we can see and touch creation and allow it to speak to us about the Spirit. Until I could hear the rose speak its message of love to me, I was not able to pass beyond its form and allow its Creator to speak to me. All of creation runs on a divine energy that at its core is unconditionally loving. The very heartbeat of God is resonating in creation. It is ever ready for us to hear and see the hidden mystery of the Creator's love to which it points. Our work is to begin to reconcile the seen and the unseen and intertwine them within our hearts. The great need is to renew the depth of our relationship between our spirituality and the mystery of creation and to develop a keen sense of creation warming, embracing, and speaking to us. To immerse oneself in the beauty of creation, its mystery and wonder, is to come to know the God beyond and the God within."

Year in and year out, whenever God opened the time for her, Betty continued to walk in the mountains to be alone with Him in creation. Through these reflective hikes she became very sensitive to the feel and texture of the mosses, the roughness of the tree bark, the heat of the stones, the colors of the wildflowers, the coolness of the water. Every little detail was instructive.

Her favorite walk started in the lowland and crossed over a bridge on a two-rut dirt road into a quiet, serene, heavily wooded area. As she walked, she was always very aware of the little watery trails hidden in the underbrush surrounded by lush, verdant Carolina green. Often, she would take the time to trace them back to their source just so she could put her hands in the cool water and splash it on her face. She was deeply present in the moment and making spiritual connections about everything she saw. She noted how much greener the life was closer to the spring and connected that with how much richer our lives are when we stay close to the Source. She often sensed that God was speaking to her so she would stop and jot down what she heard.

> Here in the mountains in September, I am visually aware that nothing has changed. The paths that I walk are still shaded in green. The fern is lush and dense on the forest floor. The gaylax leaves are sturdy and mature from the long summer season of nourishment and growth. Many flowers are in full color and weighted with bloom. Yet, in the stillness and quiet that surround me, in the seemingly unchanged, there is a deep sense that all creation is waiting, preparing to receive the

changing of season. How do we express it? "There is a touch of fall in the air."

> Creation patiently waiting.
> Creation listening with desire and expectation.
> Creation sensing its need
> And preparing to receive.
> Creation allowing growth,
> Allowing change.

All of this speaks deeply to me, for I, like creation, need to allow space for the changes that come with each season of my life. I need to achieve creation's balance and equilibrium within my soul-life. I need creation to remind me again and again of my chosenness—that I have been uniquely set apart by God to love Him and to serve Him in the fullness of my humanity. This humanity can only move toward wholeness (holiness) as I choose to allow the seasons of my life to unfold.

There is a time to be still and a time to listen. Perhaps this is the greatest single desire of the human heart: to listen attentively to the voice of God speaking through Scripture, creation, and the joys and sorrows of the seasons of each soul.

Illumination

Waiting is one of the most difficult pieces of a deep, inner spiritual journey. We tend to want to outrun God but our growth depends on consciously letting our fear go and allowing our circumstances the space to teach us what God intends. This is hard for us because so much of our waiting is filled with anxiety and our own expectations of what should happen. Thus, it subtly becomes a way of trying to control the future as well as a way of setting us up for disappointment, discouragement, and despair. It is important to understand that waiting is not passive and fearful but active and open-ended. Active waiting is always a movement from something to something more. The secret of waiting is to be always alert, always waiting with hope, trusting that something new has been awakened within us — a work in us has begun. The desires of our hearts will be fulfilled but fulfilled according to God's perfect will and timing for our lives.

As long as we are still waiting in fear and anxiety, we will not experience growth. We will stay stuck because when we are fearful, we are disconnected from the Source. We are not trusting that whatever God brings will be exactly what we need. Open-ended waiting is filled with radical hope, trusting God's perfect love to cast out our fear, knowing that all shall be well.

This way of waiting also requires that we understand that the spiritual life can only be lived in the present moment. We live in present moment awareness by living each moment to the full—pain or joy—longing to find signs of the One we are waiting for. Living always in the future produces anxiety, worry, and fear. Living in the past produces guilt, bitterness, and regret. Many of us never get out of the past or the future and miss the gift that is in the present moment. Eternity is now. When we rush ahead to the future or shrink back into the past, we miss the hand of God, which can only touch us in the now.

If we will come to prayer and wait patiently, allowing and embracing whatever the present moment brings and living it to the full, we will begin to wake up to new ways of seeing and understanding. It is in our coming again and again that we are changed. In the waiting we will be released from our personal fears and agendas and be set free to meet others with true compassion, bringing them the gift of Christ, Himself.

Come and see,

Betty

Autumn creates space for dying.
What is left untended in the heat of summer
Needs mending in the fall. For earth and flesh
Must keep their seasons and their liturgy.

The leaves fall, fall, dried and withered things
As if from some far and distant land.
Through their barren pathways up and down I wander,
Unmasking hidden gardens of my past.
O, how long my road has been.

Down, down, into the emptiness that solitude has cast.
Where memories' wavering echo relives the residue of
Suffering,
And the gray fog of sorrow drifts. Where what is near
Seems far away, a painless vastness among the stars.

Up, up I slowly climb to heights
Where long lamenting shadows
Lay lonesome across the mountain stone.
And in the quiet stillness a melancholy roams.
Where way beyond the distant ridge I see a city white.
There the radiant face of Christ appears.
And it was wet with tears.

Autumn creates space for dying
And a broken heart for crying.

BWS

CHAPTER FIFTEEN

SORROW'S
SECRET

I become a vagrant, a wanderer in these woods,
A hermit in my meadow cave,
Warmed by the inner fire of desire,
Besieged by Him Who is at the heart of everything.
The still, sad music of all humanity, its suffering
Sings clear, close incarnate notes of hope
Embraced through faith's transcendent reason.

When she was in her midfifties, Betty entered another season of sorrow and loss. Annie Tartt had a series of strokes, and Betty was spending a lot of time in Florida taking care of her. God had prepared her well for this by giving her the grace to forgive her mother and offer her love without condition or expectation. He had mercifully allowed their reconciliation, and they had experienced such a sweet healing that Annie Tartt completely entrusted herself and all of her affairs to Betty's care. Their roles were reversed now and her mother had become childlike and dependent on her. With each stroke, she was losing more of her memory and will to live, and Betty knew it would not be long before she lost her forever.

As Betty saw it, it was grace that she could at last offer her mother the precious gift of care, gentle understanding, and a listening heart, and it was grace that Annie Tartt could receive it. To be able to offer her this kind of love, Betty had to learn to let down her defenses and meet her mother out of her own brokenness. Betty had learned to see and accept her own wounded ways with compassion and kindness, so now she was able to offer Annie Tartt that same grace. By bringing the Eternal Listener into their communion, Betty had invited a transforming Presence that radically expanded her ability to meet her mother in love and provided her with the patience to be lovingly present to her as she endured the suffering and loss that aging brings. To stay with Annie Tartt in life's final and most profound spiritual movement — the movement toward physical death — was a tremendous gift and privilege.

When Annie Tartt was stable enough and Betty could find the time, she would go back to her little house in North Carolina for a few days and hike up to her mountain meadow. She would sit for hours under a small, white pine tree that had become her favorite resting spot. It was shady there, with a magnificent view of the mountains and valley in the distance and intermittent breezes that whispered across the mountain face. She pondered the many years of pain and the difficult work of reconciliation with her mother and was deeply grateful for the love they now were able to share.

It was a bittersweet time, and Betty cried many tears. Gradually, she began to realize that all of her tears were not just for her mother. She was crying, at last, for the father and brother she had loved so much and lost so many years ago. She sat in the comforting shade of that little pine tree, leaning against the rough bark of its trunk, and let the tears flow. As she mourned, she entered the repressed recesses of her soul, uncovering more and more of the buried pain of all of her losses. She returned again and again to her grieving tree, and the tears returned again and again until her heart was, at last, emptied of its grief.

"I could not fully express the depths of my feelings about grief, loss, and the deep, deep things of my life. They were unspeakable. We never get over our losses totally, but it is important to grieve them. I had to find a grieving place and take the time to sit there long enough to let the feelings come so I could identify them, embrace them, and let them bring me to tears, emptying me and waking me up to feeling again.

"I embraced my pain by bringing it into myself, reliving all of the memories, weeping and crying and reflecting. What I found when I did this was that there was so much love in the grief and that love began to heal me. The depth of the grieving process put something in me that I was not even aware of until, all of a sudden, a sweetness came up and pressed itself into my soul. The sense of the presence of my loved one's spirit was with me spilling over into tears because of the love that we shared for one another. It was a birthing of a deeper place in the love of Christ. It was in the cracks of my brokenness that the light came in.

"Grieving is a process that goes on all the time. Life is always changing, and we are always in the process of dying and having to let go. Suffering is always with us, but if we will stop running and allow ourselves to fully feel the pain of our losses, we will come in touch with a new life, a Love that is underneath the suffering. It is a Love that we were not even aware was there. The question is, can we taste that new life in the midst of our suffering? Can we see in the experience of our losses that we are being prepared for a deeper love? In the darkest of times, in terrible circumstances and calamities, in the most mundane of human realities, if we sense that we are in the Presence of God and a Love we have not yet fully tasted, we will find hope. There is solid ground under our pain: Christ, the Redeemer. We can only ascend as far as we descend to the Ground on which we can stand. From this place comes the Love that heals the world."

The enduring, the gradual losing
of one so deeply loved
brings sadness to my heart.
The shadows of a lifetime
race across my mind.
Yet, out of this pain comes beauty
for life's shadows cast in evening
are long, are strong, are lasting.
They lift and free the hurting heart
from inner thoughts of self.
They lead it forward, upward, onward
toward God's Eternity.

This deep grieving emptied her heart of its burden, making even more space that could now be filled by God. By not allowing the fear of overwhelming pain to keep her from deeply experiencing her grief, she was finally releasing all the emotions still encased in her heart from the icy numbness that had separated her from herself, from God, and from others.

The hope she now knew was that she was not alone in her sorrow. God, in watching His only Son's agonizing death, had experienced all of the grief, pain, and loss that she had and was suffering with her. She relaxed into the flow of her tears, allowing them to soften and empty her heart, gently accepting the reality of all that God had brought into her life. From this new place, she could compassionately shoulder the sorrow of others, bringing her into the tender intimacy of Christ's suffering and the depths of the meaning of hope and shared humanity.

"When I met hope, in my fifty-fifth year, on the southward side of a high mountain in North Carolina, it was unmistakable. 'Now abideth faith, hope and love.' Hope, for many years of my spiritual journey, was overshadowed by faith and love. Love's relentless wooing had won me with its unspeakable beauty, mystery, and grace. Faith became the 'yes' within me on which I slowly began to stake my whole life, while hope remained invisible and elusive. Faith and love built my self-confidence until I broke inside, then faith began to fade and love dimmed. It was in my despair that I met hope. It was in the suffering, wounded, and broken places of my life that hope began to come out of the shadows and bring me to wholeness. It was in the emptiness and stillness between faith and love, in the hollow of a heart carved out by despair, that hope took hold.

"What I realized on that unforgettable day was that hope had always lingered in the shadows of my darkest times. What awakened within me was that precisely when faith crumbles and love dims, hope begins. Hope is not the same thing as optimism. Rather, hope is the certainty that something makes sense, is worth the cost, regardless of how it might turn out. Hope is a sense of what might yet be. Hope is precisely what I had when I had nothing. It strains ahead, seeking a way behind, through, and beyond every obstacle. Hope does not try to determine how God's way will be shown but remains open to new and astonishing manifestations of God's presence at work in the circumstances of life. The more difficult the circumstances, the deeper the hope. This is the delight in despair."

> *Hope is the elusive one,*
> *Virtue's constant coming*
> *Into darkness, desolation and despair*
> *Where faith lies crumbling*
> *And love is dimming.*
> *Attentive, grace-filled, silent,*
> *Spinning, spinning, spinning.*

"I had to learn to trust the darkness of new birth and the darkness of death's desolation. I didn't always see it but new life was being birthed; it was underneath the darkness and the pain. By trusting this Ground underneath, I began to find so much hope that there was no longer the need to run or the possibility of hiding. Pain was the Voice of Love calling me home. My work was to get in touch with that Love in hope and trust. If I had resisted or run away, it would only have deepened my pain and created more for other people. My real work was to stop my resistance and be willing to go through the pain of inner death before the end of my physical life. What was dying was my false self.

"I had no inkling of it at the time, but as I persevered and slowly began to experience the glory that followed the pain, I realized that I was becoming a tremendous encouragement for others. I had compassion for them because I had suffered too, and my stony heart had been broken to allow love to enter. I was able to encourage them to use their suffering to end their suffering. He had used my pain to teach me. God created us in love, and He longs to recreate us in mercy. This process can be severe, but it is also merciful because it brings us finally to a place of deep love and acceptance. Our pain and our cross can and will speak to the wounded hearts of others in God's time and in His way. This is fertile suffering. Transformation happens if we are willing to walk the way of the cross."

Betty was being prepared for a completely new understanding of love as she sat and looked at her pain and felt it during those summers under the grieving tree. She was getting in touch with a new life that she never even dreamed was possible, a life filled with the fullness of Christ Himself. She was waking up to the transcendent mystery that the cup of sorrow and the cup of joy cannot be separated. She didn't understand it; she didn't even try because she had long before let go of needing to have all the answers. She was simply endeavoring to allow space for God to provide them in His time.

It was becoming clear to her during this period that another loss was looming: It was time to give up her beloved Old Still. She had envisioned living there for the rest of her life, but as was his pattern, Bryant had accomplished all he thought needed to be done there and was restless and ready to move on. At the same time, she could see that her mother, who lived on the other side of town, needed her more and more, so she began to pray. The process took almost three years, but in July of 1986, Betty let go. They moved to a little condo near Annie Tartt and Betty spent the next five years tending to her mother's needs. In 1991, at the age of 86, Annie Tartt went to be with the Lord.

After Annie Tartt's death, Betty spent more and more time in the mountains. Every day she would pack her worn red rucksack with her favorite water bottle, her rain gear, her whistle, her weathered compass, a clean cloth for washing her face in the streams, a piece of fruit, Brie, a few crackers, three Hershey miniatures, a stubby red pencil, a carefully folded piece of paper to write on and, of course, a book that she felt God wanted her to read. The weather never thwarted her regimen — rain or shine she climbed the mountain. If an afternoon lightning storm came through, she knew better than to stop under a tree, so she would instinctively seek cover under a cavelike rock with a little overhang. She would sit there, watching the rain, pondering how long the rock might have been there and the wisdom the years had brought to that place, relating it all to abiding in the shelter of the Almighty. She began to call these little shelters her cleft rocks.

"All of these storms and every little thing, whether it was the soft mist on the fern, the tiny rivers the cleansing rain made in the earth, or the warmth of the sun as it came through the trees to highlight just one little spot of earth — whatever it was — there was always a sense of Presence, a sense of God manifesting Himself to me through creation. I was very sensitive to all of it. I would follow a mountain stream to listen to what the rapids had to say, being very careful not to step on any of the wildflowers, and I would stop to feel the soft texture of the mosses. Even the stones were giving me many messages. And what were they saying? 'Come rest a minute, and I'll interpret God's love to you as my warmth enfolds you. I love you, I love you, I love you.' All beauty says that. Beauty speaks to us of mystery and wonder. The wonderful thing is that there is nothing fearful in all of this because there are no conditions in creation. It doesn't ask for anything, it is totally free to love us back. If we look at anything long enough, we will rejoice in the miracle of love. It's just a beautiful connection between the mystery of God and the mystery of creation. In this space, from this place, everything begins to merge — everything.

"The sound of beautiful music touches our soul and brings us together to a higher place just for a moment. Certain smells and sights connect us with our memories and reassure us of the continuity of time and the constancy of creation. The sweet smell of a tree is good. The feel of its bark is good. The sight of its sheltering strength is good. The sound of the wind ruffling its leaves is good. It is all good. God is total goodness, and these moments bring us in touch with Him and the oneness of all things. We all have a deep sense that there is much, much more to life than the way our ego is asking us to live it, but when we are given glimpses of the reality awaiting us, we tend to miss them because we are so busy. The more we pay attention, and the more we desire to move into this divine world, the more of these moments we will have, and finally the Light will break through."

> *O Love, where are all my yesterdays?*
> *I often rest in wonder.*
> *Could all my yesterdays be caught*
> *Between my finite eyes?*
> *The mountain . . . mine,*
> *The meadow . . . mine,*
> *The forest and its daybreak sky,*
> *The whisper of the wind-touched leaves,*
> *The freedom of the dipping bird,*
> *The gold dust of the stars,*
> *All mine to look at when I pleased.*
> *Such news*

Would break my heart with praise.
Such beauty, blind my gaze.
O Love, where are all my yesterdays?

"On one of my walks, I began to wonder what kind of wood the cross might have been made of. I picked up a piece of old dry wood on the trail. It had turned gray and was rather pithy and soft, and I carried it with me most of the day. It came to me as I was sitting and eating my lunch that there was no way the cross could have been made out of dry wood because it wouldn't have held the nails. So I picked up another piece of wood that I call greenwood. It was sturdy and strong and I realized that the cross would have been made out of rather freshly cut greenwood. What sort of tree it was, I didn't know, but the picture came to me as I was sitting there that the sap from the greenwood, if the nails were driven into the cross, would naturally have mingled with His bleeding. Quite suddenly and unexpectedly, I found myself caught up in this overwhelming sense of being drawn into the cross. I was profoundly experiencing it and I was removed from the temporal world. I was drawn into the magnificence of transcendence and I beheld His glory just for a moment."

Illumination

The transformation we all long for occurs in the intimate embrace of our Divine Lover, in the still, hidden places of our soul. It is here that we become real—the authentic self that God created. Becoming real is an unlearning, the process of emptying ourselves of all that we have clung to and been conditioned to by our culture. As we gradually do this painful work of emptying ourselves of our ego, illusions, and perceptions we begin to see reality, and in seeing reality we become real.

In the emptying, we are creating a holy vacancy in our souls allowing God to fill it with Himself. We are detaching from our mind's control over our lives just long enough to open a tiny gap where Spirit can touch spirit, where we can begin to hear the Voice of Love speaking to us. It is in this holy vacancy that we encounter Love, listen to the Voice of Love, and celebrate the Presence of Love. This Love is the center and source of our spiritual life and this Voice has a new and deeper message, one we must begin to trust. As we allow this holy vacancy—this little pool that is our hearts—to be filled up with the River of Living Water, our lives will naturally begin to overflow in blessing to others.

Love gently comes in, enlarging our soul and filling the emptied space with the Spirit of God, the fullness of Christ. More and more, as we empty ourselves of self, we experience God's presence surrounding us. It is something beyond expression, a sweet moment of belonging to everything, a sense of the fullness of God's love being returned to us by every created thing: the people in our life, the trees, the flowers, and all of the earth. This is the abundant life, the Divine Spirit of Love filling our emptiness. We can live in this place now—we don't have to wait for heaven. The choice is ours, right here, right now.

This journey is a process. To empty ourselves of all we think we know and move from our head into our hearts, where our spiritual life can bloom, requires very intense, intentional, prayerful longing. Only as we are able to move to this new and deeper experiential knowledge of Christ within do we begin to know the sense of mystery and wonder that transcends the intellect. Our finite minds cannot comprehend the infinite God. In the letting go of our own opinions, we gradually begin to see God as Jesus sees Him, rather than as we have created Him. This is mystery, this is transcendence, this is wonder, this is beauty.

The Spirit of Love is moving us in Christ toward the Father, into the arms of His loving Abba. He wants us to share in the beautiful, intimate relationship that is going on all the time between the Father and the Son. As we move with Him, we are moving toward oneness with God in and through everything. Eventually we begin to understand that nothing is separated. God created everything and He loves it all. If we can see all people and all things in that light, we can begin to love unconditionally and bring healing and reconciliation to the world. This is the work of emptying. Love is being birthed in us.

It is my fervent prayer that these words, which have filled the emptiness in my heart, might touch and fill the emptiness in yours and that together we might embrace all things and all people with God's love.

Betty

I, struggling, burdened, and in pain,
>day in, day out, I came
>so weighted, so chained,
>so imprisoned in my fears,
>I came to His altar
>to make my sacrifice,
>in faith, to try to die, yes, I.
Why? I know not why.
>One word will do. Love.
>It wooed me, it drew, it compelled me.
>Its simplicity seemed to fill,
>to warm, to free me.

And so I came day after day after day.
>I came in love to His altar
>to make my offering.
I offered me.
Then, alas one day, my love's piercing
>penetrated His altar
>And took me way beyond
>to heights, to depths,
>to lengths, to breadths
>to one cross made of green wood
>sap running, mingling
>with His bleeding.
I knew then that I was dying.
>For I, yes, even I,
>I beheld His Glory
>There, hanging on the green wood
>I saw Him.

BWS

Chapter Sixteen

Mystery
and Wonder

When she returned home, the flowering of Betty's true self began to reveal itself in deeper and more encompassing ways as she emptied herself more and more to follow the leading of the Spirit. She had done so much inner work: naming her fears, moving against her compulsions, grieving her losses, surrendering to Love, yet God seemed to be saying to her that there was even something more for her to discover on her quest for the high places. He would use the great contemplative writers to help her find it.

Betty's sister, Missie, began to send her books by many of the Catholic contemplative writers such as Teresa of Avila and John of the Cross. Missie had never read the books herself but sent them thinking that Betty might be interested. Betty had no idea what a contemplative even was because of the very structured religious tradition she had grown up in, but she took *Contemplative Prayer* by Thomas Merton up the mountain with her for one full summer. Though she didn't understand a lot of what it meant, she kept trying. She would write down any confusing or unfamiliar words, and when she came back down to the mountain house, she would look them up in the dictionary and try to discern the depths of their meaning. Many of the other books Missie sent sat on her bookshelf because she thought she wasn't ready for them.

"One of the books my sister mailed me was *Revelations of Divine Love* by Julian of Norwich, but I didn't read it because the title sounded a little spooky. At that point in my spiritual journey, I had a very deep sense that prayer was absolutely imperative if I wanted to be able to hear every detail of what God wanted me to do. I had begun a little regimen of getting up every morning about 6:00 to pray and watch the sun rise. Often, the Spirit of God would wash over me in these sweet times and the tears would flow. The Presence was very profound, and I could hardly wait to get up to be with Him again. One morning during my prayer, I said, 'Lord, I've got these two weeks, Bryant is gone, and there's nobody here. What do You want me to do with the time?' I walked over to my bookshelf trying to discern as best I could which book He wanted me to take to the mountain that day. The Holy Spirit seemed to be pressing me to take Julian's book, which was her personal account of experiencing God in sixteen 'showings' she had been given. I made the choice to trust that and put the book in my rucksack and headed to the mountain."

> *My prayers infused with Presence*
> *My Wardrobe of the Lord.*
> *And in my emptied hand*
> *a mystic pressed a Kingdom*
> *I so longed to understand.*

It has been said that, when the student is ready, the teacher will come, and now Betty was ready. She had spent countless hours sitting in what she called her meadow, the beautiful, open grassy space on top of Rock Mountain where her grieving tree stands. After the long pull up, it is a wonderful respite spot but it is also right on the beaten path. There are always hikers passing through, so she began to look for a place where she could be alone and read out loud. As she walked along, trying to discern from God where to go, she turned off the trail about halfway down the south face of the mountain. She passed through a brushy patch of rhododendrons and came out onto a broad, flat rock with a magnificent view of the valley and neighboring mountain. There was an old white pine tree that had been struck by lightning still clinging to the rock. The branches hung low and provided shade for the hot summer days. That day the air was warm and clear and there was a light breeze, so she sat down in the soft pine needles that cushioned the rock, opened Julian's book, and began to read out loud. She read it over and over again, trusting God to interpret its essence to her. She returned to that hidden place over and over again and the more she returned, the more God taught her through Julian and the more precious her relationship with her saintly friend became. She loved her little hideaway and it became very sacred to her. Later she named it Julian's Rock.

"Julian of Norwich was a fourteenth-century anchoress who lived in England during the Crusades and the Black Plague in Europe. At the age of thirty, she received sixteen revelations from God and then spent the rest of her life getting them down on paper. She lived in a small anchorage attached to a corner of the church. One window of the anchorage opened into the church so she could take the sacraments and the other window opened out into the world, so people could come to her for spiritual direction. In fourteenth-century England, there were no psychologists, so these anchors and anchoresses served that purpose. And so, as I approached Julian's Rock, I would see myself coming to her window to glean her wisdom.

"Summer after summer, day after day, I returned to Julian's Rock. I read everything I could about Julian and was deeply impressed by her simplicity. Julian had such a tender and intimate relationship with the Beloved that with sweet humility she would always preface the things she wrote about

God with, 'As I understand it,' and she would refer to Him as 'our courteous Lord.' While pondering a tiny hazelnut in her hand, she experienced a simple yet profound awareness: God created it, God loved it, and God would care for it. Julian understood with a knowing beyond knowing that He would do no less for her: He created her, He loved her, and He would care for her. I learned from her that every circumstance in my life would work together for good whether it felt good or not. God reassured both of us by saying to her, 'I may make all things well, I can make all things well, I will to make all things well, and I shall make all things well. And you yourself shall see that all manner of things shall be well.'[4]

"Julian's descriptions of Christ as He was dying on the cross were intensely vivid. In one of the showings, she heard Jesus tenderly saying to her, 'Julian, have I died enough for you? If I could suffer more for you, I would.' Her revelations taught me to see that everything is the voice of Love, even unspeakable pain. Pain got my attention, brought me to the end of myself, and led me home to God. Without the pain, I would never have been pressed to engage in this spiritual journey that finally led to such joy and gratitude. Our Father tenderly loves me. He is in control of my reality, so my reality, however it may look to me, is always good. Whatever is, is good. There is a huge freedom in understanding that. As Julian so sweetly summed it up, 'Then we can do no more than look at Him rejoicing, with a noble, powerful desire to be entirely made one with Him — to be centered in His dwelling, rejoicing in His loving and delighting in His goodness.'[5] Julian taught me that. She was very real to me. She was my mentor. She still is.

"Year after year, I sat there and pondered all that God was teaching me. I sat there in the sunshine, in the cold, or in the rain. It didn't matter; I watched it all. I watched as the raindrops splashed up off the rocks, returning to God, and got in touch with the descending and ascending way. I couldn't possibly ascend to God unless God first descended to me. My part was just to be open enough to receive Him. I had to be humble enough to descend with Him through my pain to the ground beneath on which I could stand before I could hope to ascend with Him to the higher places. If I had been afraid to persevere to the solid ground, I would have stayed stuck in the muddy bitterness of my pain. He has descended into me. I have descended through the pain. Now I can ascend with Him.

"As I sat there and watched that old pine tree disintegrate, I thought a lot about my own dying — not physical dying but the inner process of dying to all that I had been clinging to. All of the listening, the surrender, the trust, and the obedience was finally bringing me to the center of the reality of God — which is Love. I can't explain exactly how this understanding came about, but reading Julian affirmed me in it again and again.

"I probably spent three summers reading, pondering, and rereading Julian's book before I began to really grasp it. I would take one of her chapters or even a sentence or phrase, and I would read it over and over, thinking about what it might mean. If I had read Julian any earlier in my journey, I don't think I could have understood her. It took all the preparation of Scripture study and reading the great evangelical writers to bring me to that place. As I studied the Gospels, and now as I pondered Julian's revelations, it so spoke to me that these people were just ordinary people like me, struggling and suffering and seeking and searching, and yet they had been given the gift of the experiential knowledge of Christ, so perhaps I could be given that gift too."

> *Dear Redeemer, I long to gather*
> *The blooms from each lovely flower*
> *And scatter their petals in the dew*
> *At the feet of Your Calvary.*
> *I would so like to reach up*
> *And dry Your tears.*
> *Please know my sighs, my sorrows,*
> *My joys, my little sacrifices*

Given in flames of love.
> *These are my spring flowers,*
>> *my petals in the dew.*

"The beauty of Julian's Rock so woke me up to the mystery and the beauty and the wonder of God, that summer after summer after summer I returned to that place. All of these truths came alive to me as I returned again and again. It's so important to establish physical places in our lives where we have experienced the Presence. These places become sacred, and we return there to ask God to intensify our desire for Him. Jesus picked a beautiful place to pray the night before He was handed over to His passion. I think, after reflecting on this, that Jesus had been to the Garden of Gethsemane many times for prayer. I went to the Garden when I traveled in the Holy Land. It is a beautiful olive grove with old, old trees gnarled with age. It is a sacred place where the intensity of the Presence of the Father is still very, very real.

"My own sacred place was a pretty easy climb for me when I was younger, but now I am no longer able to make it up there. I'm deeply grateful, though, that God has given me the precious gift of memory, because I can always go to Julian's Rock in my memory and feel His sweet Presence there. So I close my eyes now and I am there — right there."

O Christ,
> *long have I sensed Your call*
> *amid it all.*
Journeyed, tired and lonely
> *in foreign lands.*
Dared to walk through midnight places
> *of guilt and fear and shame,*
> *of rejection and of pain.*

But You, known now as never before.
Mine, the gift, the ordination of
　Your piercéd hands.

Betty continued to immerse herself in books by the great spiritual writers and found great comfort in the realization that so many of them were drawn to solitude as she was. Thomas Merton, author of *Contemplative Prayer*, spoke of the "solitaries" and distinguished between the "active and the contemplative." A *contemplative* is simply a person who is deeply attentive to the Spirit's mysterious movement and who is drawn to cultivating this Presence in solitude and silence. *Solitaries* are seldom accepted in our culture, and certainly Betty had felt this rejection. These books helped her realize that she, too, had been created as a contemplative by God and that it was okay. She was at last being affirmed in and living out of who she was created to be. Her contemplative journey had finally brought her to the precious discovery of her true self and the profound gift of the experiential knowledge of God — divine union.

Love gone wild
Love gone free
Love come alive in me.
Self-emptying, self-giving, rejoicing
Ecstasy expanding me.

Red flower sunset
Floating into eternity
Reaching back, touching me
The door blown open
The dancing soars
All is given, all is poured.

Underneath the suffering, the pain
A white stone, a new name
A smile, an etching
Pure grace, holy joy
The Beloved's face.

"I was awake at last and everything changed. I saw with new eyes, new proportions, new depths, and new light, and I sensed a Presence and warmth of knowing that I was deeply loved. I was a solitary, and God was affirming me, telling me that He loved and created me that way.

"If we persevere in our desire and commitment to live our life in love, the best will be given to us. It is almost impossible to put words around, but slowly and imperceptibly, this experiential relationship with the Beloved begins to express itself and we begin to sense the Presence in our work and in our prayer. When that transition happens, we are abiding always in the Presence. That is the ultimate end of the journey, as far as we can have an ultimate end on this earth. As I sensed that more and more, I yearned to be alone with the Beloved. Love was drawing me, wooing me. I was enthralled and mystified by Love, and in the depths of my being, I wanted to see the face of the Beloved. Very much like Peter on the Mount of Transfiguration, everything in me wanted to pitch a tent and stay in that place alone with the Beloved forever. But, like Peter, I knew that He was asking me to push against my longing and offer what I had learned on the mountain to the wounded hearts of others."

Illumination

As I slowly walked into the beauty that is God and began to wake up to see and hear differently, I began to have a sweet sense of divine intimacy. Jesus came into the world and gathered all of our joy and our suffering and sorrow into His tender embrace. Drawn by the Spirit with Jesus into God, the ultimate end of our journey is this intimate union with God. It is gradual and very difficult to speak about, but once we have a sense of His abiding presence, our loneliness turns to sacred solitude. We are alone but we are walking with Someone: Emmanuel, God with us.

Our spiritual journey is a love affair. It is a leaning into God, listening longingly for His heartbeat. Our breathing becomes synonymous with the Breath of Life and brings us into harmony with the divine flow of life. It is a transcendent resting in, being with, and living in the Presence all of the time.

Solitude, silence, and listening bring us into this intimacy. In deep silence, we see and let go of the things that have separated us from the Holy One. This intimate relationship can and must transcend the structure we have depended on in our spiritual journey up to this point. As deeply spiritual people who are longing for the great plateau of freedom that God offers, we are finally asked to put aside for a while all of the sacred but tangible and intellectual aspects of the journey and fall in love again with the Beloved. We are abiding, resting in God alone. In 1 Corinthians 2:2, Paul says, "For I resolved to know nothing while I was with you except Jesus Christ and him crucified."

I find that where I am now in my own journey, I don't seem to want anything much anymore but to be quiet and listen to the Voice of the Beloved. In a sense, I think I am hearing the music of heaven and that Voice is so sweet it brings tears to my eyes.

Could it be that such a love, His love, is all the answer we really need?

Betty

Out of the earth rise the mountains.
From the rim of the meadow, withered with moss,
Rises the falcon in his feathered cloth.
Through the soft rain, mist glistening like mica,
The quilts of wildflowers begin again.

When I die, I would like to die
On a day of mist and mica and of rain.
Descending rain, ascending rain, endless rain,
The kind I know will never end.

My ceremony,
One of shoveled ashes,
Shoveled out into the sky,
Free of sorrow and the pain of letting go,
Free to soar to heights
Like the falcon in his feathered cloth.

And anyone who comes
Must travel inward silently
With thoughts of destination.
Death's preparation —
A place called Julian's Rock.

BWS

Chapter Seventeen

Love's Fire

I am a February child
Born in winter's season.
I came to earth, no choice, I was misdirected
In a month of silver spirits and of snows.
The cold of winter is not all I know.
I have traveled all life's seasons.
Awakening springs and pain-filled summers,
And now, His peace in autumn.
Yet I cannot say with any reason
Which season Wisdom entered in.

Betty felt a deep yearning to communicate her intimate encounters with the Divine. The great saints of Scripture wrote, "We tell you this because we have experienced it," and "We tell you this that our joy may be complete." John of the Cross, Julian, and Teresa of Avila all labored to write about their experiential knowledge of God. Very often they spoke of it through poetry, because the mystery is so profound that it just cannot be held in simple prose.

It is Betty's burden and gift to testify to the still small Voice that called her and is always calling to us through the noise and din of life, exhorting us to play our part in the vast and beautiful symphony He is creating in the universe of time. She has paid the price and done the arduous work of interior transformation so the Spirit could touch the spirit of those God would put on her path. Now she encourages others to wake up, to look deep within themselves to see what is separating their heart from the heart of God so they might have the experiential knowledge of union with God—the gift of the Giver Himself—which is for anyone and everyone. This is her sacred call.

"I thought about all that Jesus suffered by entering the world. The fullness of God in the precious, tender, broken body of Christ: the Incarnation. Sometimes I felt such an intense longing to be with the Beloved that the separation became painful. As I saw it, though, I could not just completely detach and be a hermit hidden from the world. Jesus told His dear friend, Peter, to demonstrate that he loved Him by feeding His sheep and that same love was compelling me. Love can be kept only insofar as it is given away. If my life was going to speak for God, it had to speak in the place where He had put me. And the place He had put me in was an affluent world of productivity and 'Let's get it done' and 'Who has time to stop and meditate?'

"Now, in the twilight of my years, I feel very pressed to encourage people who are on their spiritual journey to persevere, to trust God, and not stop short of the goal—the gift of the Giver Himself, divine union. The gates of heaven are everywhere. Our part is to simply embrace and open to each new season of our inner and outer journey as preparation to receive this gift of Love. Divine union is for everyone, and the experiential knowledge of this Love and freedom is everything. At last, we are grasped by the hand of the Spirit and led into a wilderness free of distractions and temptations, a wilderness of trackless mystery, beauty, and sound. This is the Ultimate Food in the feast of our redemption—a foretaste of heaven. Once we have tasted it, there is no turning back. It gets sweeter and sweeter. It is a freedom that comes from a wisdom that transcends the intellect; it is an un-knowing, a letting go of all we have known and falling deeply in love with God in whose heart we will finally find rest. If we will do this, our soul will expand to the point that we draw all humanity into it, and in the process there will be peace in our heart, joy in our life, and reconciliation and healing among our friends and family. This journey is costly and it is sacrificial, but this Love is healing and brings with it the gift of sanctity. I can't explain it, but it is so."

> *My Beloved.*
> *Simple union*
> *Is the fullness of life.*
> *Since the day of my yielding*
> *I have known love, peace, and light.*
> *I shut my eyes*
> *And I cry.*
> *Within me a hidden, infinite Beauty,*
> *Decades of charted and uncharted sighs.*
> *I am struck by Your spirit of quest.*

So Betty came down from her mountain and dared to begin to offer in the valley some of what she had learned. She was in her sixties now, with the same strong desire for privacy, but in faith and trust and determination, she moved against that, as well as her fear of the work involved and her fear of rejection. She had reached out to many people in the past but had been frequently rejected. Once, she mailed a book to a friend but when she went to get her mail several days later, the book had been returned unopened. It felt like a knife in her heart and she just sat down on the pavement and cried. The pain was not just the rejection, but the fact that what she so longed to offer would not be received. So moving against that fear and daring to reach out again took a tremendous amount of courage and trust.

The first person she invited to come to the mountain was her sister. She told her that she would like to have a spiritual retreat rather than just a friendly visit, and Missie was surprisingly open to that. Betty explained the plan for their time together that she sensed God was calling her to. Each morning they would meet in the living room in silence to watch the sun rise over the mountain. Then they would pray as the Spirit led and read *My Utmost for His Highest*. Afterward, they would walk up the mountain, keeping a little distance between them so they were away from each other enough to hear from God rather than each other. When they got to the top, they would share what they had seen and heard and felt on the walk up.

Betty was so amazed when Missie enjoyed the retreat that weeks later when God pressed Betty to reconnect with an old friend who had been in one of her youth groups as a teenager, she had more courage. In obedience, her hand shaking as she picked up the phone, Betty fought thoughts of rejection and invited her young friend to come to the mountains for a retreat. She gave her the exact time and dates and explained with absolute clarity the format they would follow and was again surprised when she agreed to come. Even more surprising to her was that when her friend came, she was not only listening intently to what Betty was saying but seemed to be hungry for it and deeply moved by it.

They spent a wonderful day on the mountain together. They walked separately but stopped about halfway up to rest and talk for a little while. Betty took her to her sacred place, Julian's Rock, and they read some from a book and just sat there together for a long time. Her friend was unusually quiet. On the way home, Betty was pretty far behind, and as she approached a beautiful grassy clearing at the bottom of the mountain, she heard her friend call out to her. She was sitting there in the warm fall sunshine waiting for Betty, very relaxed and rested, as if to say, "Let's just sit together one more time before this day is over in the mountains." Later that evening, she told Betty she had no idea that the kind of intimacy with God she witnessed that day was even a possibility.

"I was so surprised that people were actually listening and responding to what I had to say. I had tried so hard to minister to people in the past and had experienced so much rejection, but as I came more and more in quiet to receive the Love, I discovered that I had much, much more to offer. The Love that was filling me began to overflow and spill over into my world and touched people's hearts.

"This is just as I see it, but when the gift of the Giver is imparted, it seems that there is a power also imparted. Your life and words begin to touch others in a whole new way. It is a tremendous mystery, but in time, when you have done the arduous work of emptying yourself of self, God senses that you are finally ready to receive this trust. I have reflected on how long I have desired this and how long it took me to receive the gift. In great humility, I would say that I think God has a sense that this power cannot be misused and when this person can be trusted to use it to glorify the Son and, through Him, in the Spirit, to glorify God and bless many, many others.

"It is all about acceptance. Are we going to allow God to draw us into Himself? Are we willing to let go of our old trapeze and do our work of naming, claiming, and taming our demons? Are we willing to face the darkness of the tomb? If we are, God finally grants us the wonderful opportunity to look back at our lives—and retrospect is such a beautiful view—and say, 'Aha! So this is what that was about!'"

> *O quest*
> *Here*
> *In my place of secret wooing*
> *No fear disturbs my peace*
> *No clutter drapes the door*

Life, a Living Temple
Drifts slowly across a timeless shore
Light, a shimmering image
Love, an endless dance

Beyond all knowing of ever knowing
I know
That what is real is real only for one time
Only for one place
And all I have is Now

Gradually, more people came to the mountain. They were from all different walks: evangelical, Catholic, Episcopal, agnostic, whatever, but they were all stuck in the clutter of their personal opinions, convictions, and biases hoping for a deeper freedom. At home, more and more people began to ask to see her for one-on-one spiritual direction. They would then go out and tell their friends about how they were being impacted by this small woman with such great love. In 1993, on a trip to Israel with a group from Jacksonville, one of the women noticed that Betty was going to the chapel every morning to pray. She asked if she and a few others could join her and if she would mind preparing a reflective lesson for them before they went out to see the sights of the Holy Land. They were so touched by what they experienced as she prayed that they asked her to keep the group going when they returned home.

Word spread about this woman who knew Jesus in such an intimate way and who brought Him to life through her words, her friendship, and her unconditional love, and many people expressed a desire for more tangible tools and reminders of how to open to God's love. Betty sensed that she needed to get some of the things God was teaching her on paper and mail them out.

"I didn't consciously plan any of this. It was God at work in it all. In the Scriptures, Jesus lays out a pattern for ministry that often has been overlooked in today's success- and goal-oriented culture. Even the church has been unconsciously influenced by the world's pattern. So often, the need is identified first (ministry), then a committee is appointed to study and implement the program (community), and finally the members pray about how best to make it work (communion). But Jesus' way appears to be exactly the opposite. First, He went into the desert to pray and be alone with His Father (communion), then He called together a few people to love and spend time with (community), and then they went out to offer to the world what they had experienced in their time together (ministry).

"The sacred process of ministry is beautifully demonstrated in the Scripture. Very early in the disciples' relationship with Jesus, Luke records that they were fishing together but were not catching anything, so Jesus told them to cast their nets on the other side of the boat. When they did, they caught so many fish that their nets broke (see Luke 5:1-11). Our own nets are brimming full with His love but early in our journey we haven't yet experienced the depths of this reality, so our lives and words don't deeply touch others. We speak from our own needs, biases, and opinions rather than from a heart of love, so our nets finally break and we miss the blessings God has for us.

"The Scripture records that after the crucifixion, Peter, stricken with grief and reeling from pain, encouraged the other disciples to go back with him to Galilee to go fishing. This is where they had experienced again and again the presence of their Lord. This is where they had walked together, talked together, broken bread together — where they had learned to love one another. In the wilderness of our transformation, when we're down and feeling separated from everything, it is good to return to a place where we have experienced God. So they went back to that place and went fishing. It was all they knew to do.

"The water in the Sea of Galilee is so clear that you can see the fish from above, so it was not unusual for a person to be seen up on the high bank directing the fishermen where to cast their nets. Peter had taken his clothes off, probably trying to keep dry while throwing the casting net where the pointer was directing him. The others were in the back of the boat handling the seining net. When they pulled in the nets, they were shocked to find over 150 large fish putting an enormous strain on their nets, but miraculously, the nets held.

"Peter looked again and recognized that this was not just an average pointer; it was the risen Lord. So, he put his clothes back on and jumped in the water and swam to the beach. In this sweet story, the risen Lord had prepared a little breakfast for His friends on the beach. Their hearts were now ready; their eyes and their ears were now open to see and to hear and understand on a whole new level what He would say to them. Jesus asked Peter, 'Do you love me? Do you love me? Do you love me?' and Peter, finally at the place that he really knew and trusted this love, said, 'Lord, you know all things and you know that I love you.' Then Jesus said to Peter, 'Because you now know this love, you've experienced this love, you believe this love, you're present in this love, go feed my sheep with His love. Your nets will hold' (John 21:1-19, Betty's paraphrase).

"Jesus says that the pure in heart will see God, but becoming pure in heart doesn't happen the minute we say we accept Christ in our lives. When we do that, the work is just beginning. Again and again we fall, we fail, our nets break. The important thing is to accept the fact that we are broken people who are going to fail but that Jesus will mend our nets. When we allow God to empty us of self and refill us with Himself, our nets will hold the immeasurable blessing of the fullness of Christ and our lives will overflow in nourishment to others."

Beloved
It's different now from then
When fear and darkness reigned
And I was framed in pain

My soul starved
All spokes turned inward
The hub was gone.

Beloved
You looked with love upon me
A gaze which blazed its way into my heart
Imparted grace
A thread of hope illuminated my darkness
Such mercy slowly set me free.

"Looking back on my ministry years, I realize that my life only began to speak when the channel of my heart was finally clear enough of myself for God's love to flow through me unhindered. I was learning to simply listen in love to what these people had to say. To stay with this kind of intensive listening took infinite patience. It was much more than hearing words; I wanted to feel where the words came from and be aware of God's presence in our communication. In deep communion with Him, I realized I was actually listening others into the Eternal Listener's presence. It goes beyond words; I had nothing to do with it. I could never fix or change or bring a person to an experience of God. God was asking me, in the sweet name of Jesus, just to be with them in their suffering, manifesting His presence to them.

"A deeply spiritual person who has, through a lifetime of pursuit, been changed into the image of Christ's likeness can help change another life. In unconditional loving, there is a gradual letting go of the illusion that we know what is best for another person. This brings with it a quiet, affirming, loving gentleness that the other feels. This love, which is the Spirit of God pouring through that person, frees people to say things that perhaps they might not otherwise share. It is a holy time of prayer in a sense, because there is such a depth of love and presence that surrounds you, bringing you into the circle of love, into an encounter with God. This is the transcendence, the Spirit touching their hearts in the midst of their pain."

> *Obscurity is the final peace.*
> *The hidden are those chosen then released.*
> *They wear no garnish amid reality, no fame.*
> *They serve unobtrusively without the noise of name.*
> *Yet peace burns through them like a flame.*

"I had no training at all in spiritual direction, so whenever someone came to see me for counsel, I would always pray that God would unravel for me the mysteries of their heart. I wanted to know and understand them better so I would be able to love them better. I spent many hours in thought and prayer for each person, trying to discern, as best I could, how I might help to relieve some of their pain. This willing, open presence and attention to every detail of their need was very important. It was touching their hearts and they, then, were going out and touching the hearts and lives of those around them.

"For a very reclusive, dyslexic person, this kind of ministry was difficult and costly, because it took so much energy to remember, ponder, and write down everything I was hearing. I thought nothing of spending an entire day writing a letter to someone I had been counseling, and I had to weave all of this into the realities of a husband, four children, and eleven grandchildren. I don't think any of it could have happened if I hadn't been given this tremendous, absolute trust that God was going to put it all together.

"The great truth that we must remember in all of this is that we cannot give away what we do not possess. If we haven't done our work of emptying and claiming all of this for ourselves, it is impossible for God to use us because our perception of truth is still cluttered with self. People are desperately struggling under the enormous weight of their crosses and they need our help. They need us to be their Simon of Cyrene. 'I will help you carry that for a while until you are strong enough, until you have found the ground of your being, until you understand this ever greater opening up to love. I will walk with you through this until the time comes when you can carry your cross alone.' So praise God for people who are willing to persevere and be present to people in their suffering, who believe with all of their hearts and who long to become one who can help another find their way home. This is what ministry is all about, helping one lonely pilgrim carry a burden until she can find her way home. It is very costly grace. It cost God everything and it couldn't cost us any less. This is ministry.

"This ministry of presence becomes an encouragement to people to persevere. Because I had embraced my own pain, I was able to lead from my weakness and offer the hope and healing I had experienced. As the Presence came through me and touched their hearts, we experienced a sweet communion, but above everything it was confirming and arousing what was deepest within them—hope.

"As more people came, I pictured in the Scriptures how Jesus would come down from the mountain and find a 'level place' to stand on to teach the people. I thought, 'Well, I think I have found some sort of level ground that is the ground of my being, so maybe it is okay to start teaching what I have learned.' So I started that little community, and every Friday morning people would come in and we would just love each other and give each other a big hug. I would also do a few retreats. Those were wonderful years."

Those were wonderful years, but God was not through with her yet.

Illumination

We are asked to keep our focus on the majesty, the mystery, and the wonder of the Trinity—God in three persons—and the supreme virtues of faith, hope, and love. The Father gives us faith to know that we are truly His beloved. The Son gives us hope for the possibility of our redemption and the Holy Spirit brings us into love. We must be drawing these supreme virtues consistently into our inner and outer life. Are we walking in faith? Are we clinging to hope? Do we desire to learn how to love? Working interdependently, faith, hope, and love are the means that bridge the infinite distance between God and His creatures. As we merge with these virtues and begin to draw from them, we grow into the likeness of Christ and become a blessing to others.

First, we must accept in faith the gift of our creation by God — that He loves us with an unspeakable, unconditional, never-failing love. He loves us regardless of our brokenness and He will take care of us. Until we claim this gift of our belovedness — until it is truly ours — we cannot give it to others. "I have claimed my belovedness. Now I want to help you claim yours." This is what ministry is all about.

This faith will lead us to hope in the second great acceptance, which is the possibility of our redemption through Christ. Our minds are just not capable of comprehending that the infinite, transcendent God could love us so much that He would be willing to send His Son to suffer and die to make this possible. Even the ugliest, most painful, and negative things in our lives can be redeemed and used. Nothing is ever wasted. Everything works together for good, through the gift of Jesus Christ. This is a marvelous way of thinking and truly a gift. We can be grateful for everything and that is a huge freedom; it is unspeakably precious. Not only are our sins forgiven but they can be used to teach us what we need to wake up to and bring to Him to redeem. If we will gather the crumbs of our fears and false self and bring them to the Great Redeemer, He will use them for His purposes in us. In this way, we use our suffering to end our suffering. My own suffering brought me to the One who healed me. Now, as I abide in Him, I may be living through difficult, painful circumstances, but I am not suffering.

The third gift we must accept is the gift of the Spirit in our hearts that brings us to love. It is the gift of truly belonging to God that lies underneath our awareness, immersed in darkness most of the time. When our hearts finally awaken to this gift of Love, the Spirit begins to move, changing our life and focus. We begin to realize that we can do whatever we are called to because the Spirit will enable us. We begin to open ourselves to cleansing and consecration by God.

When we contemplate the mysteries of Christ, they are overwhelming, but these acceptances are vital and have to gradually be incorporated into our spiritual journey. Conversion is not a one-time thing. It is an ongoing process that involves being born over and over again. In the processing of these virtues, we drop our illusions and attachments, accepting with joy whatever God brings into our lives, knowing that because it is, it is for our good. We come finally into the likeness of Christ and mirror His love to a pain-filled world.

Standing firm in the consoling hope that, in giving ourselves to this mystery of love, God comes.

Now is the suffering season of my years
A never ending struggle without pause.
No clarity beneath this burning gaze of age
No drenching rain to fall and cool its blaze
Only the slowed down steps
The heavy load — the cross.
Spirit of Love, a suffering love
My passion.

And though the why of aging, its mysteries still elude me
I know I do not walk this season all alone.
Into the peace of promise I slowly drift
Detached from time, age and humiliation
Immersed in cool, refreshing streams of grace
Parched lips reach up through sunlit waters
The sweetest of all praise — gratitude.
Spirit of Love, a suffering love
My passion.

Each deliberate step I take in faith
Weaves an ever clearer tapestry of Truth.
All illusions, false dreams fade
Things are as they are
The love, the joy, the peace to which I so aspire
Borne through Spirit, is mine, lives on
Only in what remains behind — my suffering.
Spirit of Love, a suffering love
My passion.

BWS

CHAPTER EIGHTEEN

THE

HIDDEN LIFE

Betty continued to send out the meditations she was writing, and oddly, she began to get a few little checks back in the mail written to Betty personally. She didn't know what to do with them as they were only sent because of something God had given her, so she had a sense that she should put them somewhere other than into paying her laundry bill. Her son, Charlie, suggested that she open a separate bank account but to do that he told her she would need a name for the account. So she took it to prayer. What kind of ministry was this really, and what was the vision for it? She thought about the fact that every time she had written one of her little meditations, she had felt the Holy Spirit pressing her not to sign it but to just "mark it." The mark she had chosen was her initials, BWS, so it seemed to her that the name on the account should simply be BWS Ministries.

The ministry was official now. The next step seemed to be to get a tax number, which was applied for and received in a miraculously short time. A dear friend who had also suffered deeply from depression and was now very well and strong became Betty's assistant, "her scribe," and helped her with all of the writings and mailings. Ultimately, there was enough money in the bank to open a small office with space for spiritual direction and groups.

There began to be so many people that Betty felt the need to organize retreats for them so that they could be together and begin to know each other at the same time that they were hearing from her. On these retreats, they watched the sun come up, being still and silent together, listening for God's movement among them. More requests for contemplative retreats, presentations, quiet days, and spiritual direction came in and she continued to teach the community that had formed. They met every Friday morning for almost ten years. It was a very costly offering that demanded a tremendous amount of time and focus, particularly at her age, but she received a tremendous amount of love in return.

Ten years later, in 2004, Betty began to sense that she just wasn't able to keep up with all of the demands of the ministry anymore. She was 78, and she could feel her energy rapidly waning. Bryant was suffering with increasingly difficult health problems, and on top of that was having a very hard time emotionally dealing with the reality of his aging. This was adding to the strain, because it was painful for her to watch this once-powerful man, still trapped in his compulsive behaviors, become debilitated by the aging process.

They had already given up the mountain house a few years earlier. That lifestyle had gotten to be more than either of them could manage, and in the spring of 2004, it became clear to her that it was time for yet another door to close. The active phase of the ministry was getting to be too much, so after much tearful prayer, she was led to close the office. She had a strong sense, too, that she was very soon going to have to give up her little condominium that she loved and go to a place where she would be able to better manage the aging process. It was yet another loss she would have to grieve. Thankfully, though, she had learned to accept and trust the fact that everything changes; nothing ever stays the same.

"The aging process is so painful because along with it comes a tremendous sense of loss, and restlessness, and a vague sense of shame, especially for those who haven't done the work of emptying themselves of ego and finding their true self during their younger years. They still think they can fix and change things by doing things the way they always did them, but now the painful limitations of physical aging make that impossible. The temptation is to deny the condition they find themselves in, but in truth it is a whole new reality that they cannot escape. As with all matters of ego, a fierce battle ensues to cling to the things that seemingly provided security, power, esteem, and control in the past, but it is a battle that no one can win—it is an illusion to try. The flesh is dying and nothing can stop the deterioration. It renders us to ashes. It is a mystery, but it is God's plan, so it will be all right.

"I will always remember when my dear, dear friend and spiritual companion was diagnosed with Alzheimer's disease. We spent many hours together, and in one of our last tearful sessions together, I was trying to encourage her. I could not identify with the fearsome pain she was dealing with of losing her mind and memory, so I simply said to her that, even though we would not be able to communicate in the temporal realm of things anymore, we needed to remember and trust that we would always be able to communicate through the Transcendent One in prayer. She was deeply relieved and grateful. The gift of the Presence was with us that day and will keep us connected forever. Our hearts are bound together in Christ's love. This is eternal truth."

> *Your voice speaks often now and clear.*
> *You are the fire of silence*
> *seeking a soundless will.*
> *You are heaven happening*
> *when my soul is still.*

"In old age, our energy slows, our eyesight weakens, and our mind may go. The physical body begins its slow, determined walk back to its Creator—a journey that can be terrifying—but if we have a sense that God is with us, we are able to endure it without fear. So I can't drive anymore—more time to rest in God. I can only eat one meal a day—that's okay, I'm grateful for that. Yes, the loss and the adjustment are painful. I know because I am experiencing it. But gratitude is everywhere. If we will see each season of our lives as preparation for the next and live it to the fullest, embracing all of it—the good and the bad—we will not miss the one changeless, transcendent fact: the Divine Love of God.

"So now at my age, I can still sit, talking, touching another life, without any condemning or controlling and feel the love flowing between us. Our spirituality is all about dying to our ego in order to enter into this giving and receiving of love. I see a picture in my heart all the time of the sweet, sweet relationship between the Father and the Son. The Father, so willing to pour Himself out for the Son and the Son so willing to receive it and give it all back—no strings, no conditions, no counting the cost. This is the relationship I longed to be drawn into and bring others into. You know, maybe it really is all about how we can help each other die, so we can help each other live."

Time grinds unrelenting
Cuts across the face of life
Burns all boundaries
Denial, resistance, all illusions
Renders us to ashes

I sit defenseless
Upon time's shore
Watch its stream flow slowly by
Silver-plated ripples

Echoes of the past
Leaving me with memories
And with longings
Like scattered stars
Undivided, paceless, without reason

Encircling all my seasons
In the fire of Holy Light
Releasing all my singing
To the darkness, to the night

"As I have experienced my own aging, I have pondered this movement toward death a lot. Our Lord endured the darkness of the tomb, and we, too, must go through our time in the tomb in some way and at some point in our lives.

"The way of trust lies through Gethsemane and Holy Saturday. Every phase of our Lord's life and every aspect of His death speak to us if we will open to it. Our time in the tomb — the wilderness — is so often the missing link in our own lives. The wilderness of our suffering is not just a place of darkness and temptation. It is the place of our transformation through which the false self must move. It is the place of conversion where the emotional pain of a lifetime, stored in the unconscious, is revealed and then gradually let go of. This is not a time of separateness, although it may feel that way. It is a time that links us to the Eternal. It is in walking through the darkness that we learn to discern the voice of the Beloved and receive the grace of interior resurrection and the capacity for divine union. All things grow in the darkness and the silence. There are hidden depths that only the Spirit can reach. It is a hidden life (see Colossians 3:3).

"This is just as I see it, of course, but it seems that during our lives we experience two of what I call tomb times. During our younger years, we may be entombed by debilitating depression, painful circumstances, or just compulsive running to avoid pain. Often times we are moving so fast that we are not even aware of our tomb until we suddenly wake up in the darkness. We become completely depleted during this time because we burn so much negative energy fighting the fear of what we are experiencing. We need to shift our focus and accept that this season of darkness is truly a time of preparation, a stilling. Acceptance of our 'not-knowing' brings forth a complete transformation of self if we will trust it. Its purpose is purification and purgation and leads ultimately to freedom—freedom to be who God created us to be, to love and live in God, and to be filled with God. If we will allow the darkness and the silence, God will allow the seeds of our false self to die just enough for Him to send up a little sprout of new life. It takes a long time for a tree to grow to its fullness, but as it emerges from the darkness, it offers shelter and beauty to the world. If we will submit to the process, be still and do the work of turning toward God and taming our demons, we will emerge from our first tomb experience with a new compassion that can deeply minister to others because enough of our self has died to allow God's pure love to shine through.

"The diminishment of the aging process takes us back into the tomb—only now the tomb is our decaying physical body. If we have not done our work of dying to our ego in the first tomb time, the aging process will humiliate it to death in this very difficult season. The beautiful reality, though, is that if we have done our work we find that we are able to enter the second tomb in complete freedom and abide there with the One we have been searching for all of our life. Now, at last, we are at rest, free of everything that kept us so fragmented and distracted in our younger years and we become totally absorbed by Him, with Him, and in Him. As Paul says, the outer man is diminishing but the inner man is being renewed and re-created (2 Corinthians 4:16, Betty's paraphrase).

"The icing on the cake is that all we have offered to others during our years between the tombs is given back to us a hundredfold. It is impossible to feel lonely in this second-tomb time because our communion with God is so deep now. The really sweet thing is that all of those we have ministered to and offered our love to go with us into the tomb in spirit and love and are a part of us forever. Now it is their time for ministry—to call others home to the heart of the Father—and our prayers sustain them in their trials and encourage them to persevere. All of this rich, warm, intimate love goes with us into the tomb of aging and on into eternity where we are always in communion with God. We are connected through Christ to one another forever. This is the joy and richness of the communion of saints. This is ministry that blooms into eternity.

"I have learned that life is a joyful dance, but we must have the courage and the hunger to step into the dance. God is the dancer. Are we going to let Him dance us any way He wants, any time, any place? It hurts sometimes, but it's part of the dance and it hurts much more if we resist. We learn by taking one step into the dance—the flow of trust—and we allow God to dance us. Then we take another and another and if we continue to take the steps, one day we start dancing and never stop. I can tell you it is so."

Forever I slept beneath the thorn
Until awakened by the golden dawn.
Forever I roamed separate and alone
Until the rainbow opened and the twilight closed.
Forever I looked to distant lands
Until my brimful eye could hold
Transforming light, a burning soul.

Mine is the wisdom tracing the spiral of a shell.
Mine is the peace that drinks from a star-filled well.
Mine is the scent of transcendence,
From the silent offering of a flower.
Mine is the gaze that blesses

From the Love of one Living hour.
Mine is the memory of all desire.
Mine is the world's ashes, its kindling fire.

Illumination

The ultimate end of our inner spiritual journey is the experiential knowledge of God—the gift of the Giver Himself. It is union with God, the infusion of His Spirit. How do any of us ever become pure enough to experience this transcendence when we are all so trapped in ourselves? How could a fearful person like me ever get there? Truly, I think the final movement is just a gift. After the last scraps of clinging to the old false self have been left behind forever, after we have done all of this work of emptying and purifying our hearts, the Holy Spirit gently and mysteriously leads us to this place in His time. When that happens, we are living from the place of what Paul calls "prayer without ceasing," and our lives begin to speak. It's mystery. It's God's divine work in us if we choose to desire it. It is all desire. As we continue to ask God to intensify our desire for Him, and as we continue to take the next step toward Him, God finally meets us in the holy vacancy in our souls and, like a beam of light, pours through our transparency and connects with our spirit, filling us with the ultimate gift: the gift of Himself in Christ.

Many, many people come to the altar, but few find their way to the foot of the Cross. Only John the beloved and the three Marys were there when our Lord was crucified—fear had scattered the rest. Jesus leads us to the foot of the Cross and then we are drawn into the Cross. There we die to all that is false and become one with Him. It is when we pass through the Cross that our hearts are softened by a profound compassion that embraces the whole world. We have finally passed through ourselves and transcended the things of the world that would keep us in bondage.

Paradoxically, all of the spiritual work and activity we have done on our journey to bring us to this place must now be let go of. Everything has to be still. Nothing is so one with the nature of God as stillness. We become completely transparent to Love like a windowpane, so clean that the Light can flow through unhindered. Empty now of our own thoughts, emotions, will, and illusions, we are in a passive state before God, completely submissive, surrendered, and receptive. We have abandoned ourselves into the hands of God. At last, the messenger has become the message. "I no longer live, but Christ lives in me" (Galatians 2:20). We see that everything in our lives—all of the pain and all of the beauty—has been woven together into the huge tapestry of divine love. The will is disciplined, the old voices are quieted, the heart is surrendered, and we hear only the voice of the Beloved saying, 'I love you, I love you, I have loved you since the beginning of time. I will not abandon you.' Pure Spirit touches pure spirit and the love of God pours through us, empowering us to give the gift of divine love to others simply by being present to them. By living in this way, we experience His presence and we transform the world from within. This is ministry. This is the healing power of Love.

Our precious Lord is setting you apart. He's calling you unto Himself to be and to become His disciple. What an honor. He has much to teach you and you have much to learn. So take His hand now, even as I am offering you mine, and in the warmth of such an all-compelling love, let us follow Him together.

I love you,

Betty

My journey is a turning, a returning,
A healing, never whole.
It is a story lived,
A story seldom told.

In desolation, dissipated, and in pain,
I roamed the dark and braided shadows of my days,
Longing for order amid my chaos,
Looking for new ways,
Searching for what belongs and where it is.

In silence and alone, I slowly struggled upward.
Above me, the hills had caught the morning Light.
I heard it singing as I went
Among the grass blades and the leaves.
I touched the grey roots of ancient trees,
Their wisdom woven in the rocks.
The dew-wet footprints in the moss are His.
I follow to the cross.
And what is heaviest and mute
Is found, is freed, is raised
In a single, silver strand of praise.

I join hands with others and the earth,
Step into this costly dance.
For eternal is the wheel and endless is the dance
That grinds the seasons of the soul
Where nothing falls but into Life.

Grace brought me to this place,
This gentle hill and ground
Where all Beauty is first found.
My story lies upon it, I rest beside it in the dark.
For what I found, I am.
And where I am is Home.

BWS

ACKNOWLEDGMENTS

One of the many gifts of this work has been a whole new friendship with and appreciation for Peter and the other disciples. There we were, two fisherwomen just sitting there trying to mend the broken nets of our lives, when God walked up and said it was time to write a book that would heal many, many hearts and, for reasons known only to Him, we were the ones to write it. Our dislocated jaws betrayed our lack of trust, so He assured us that He didn't expect us to do it alone and had already surrounded us with a host of His very best friends to help us with this awesome responsibility.

The first friend God sent was Steven Pressfield. Steve gave us our marching orders to find our muse, put blinders on, and "kick resistance in the butt." Next was Winslow Homer's beautiful painting of "Autumn." She became our muse and continually brought us back into focus. We are forever grateful for the enormous blessing of Jerry May and his precious encouragement so early on and throughout the process. Even as his health began to drain his energy, he continued to offer his profound presence. J. Philip Newell read one of our earliest and worst drafts without even knowing us and still wanted to be our friend. Phyllis Tickle kept us hoping.

Terry Behimer, our wonderful friend, brilliant editor, and God's conduit for this sacred work, had eyes to see from the very beginning. We are eternally grateful to her helping us perfect and share this gift with the world.

Becky Anderson's constant willingness to help us with her organizational gifts, endless affirmation, and quiet encouragement will always be a treasure. As Betty's closest friend, caretaker, and "scribe," she edited and cataloged all of Betty's writings that we so depended on.

Thank you to those dear friends who prayed, gave, and encouraged us.

KITTY: Cath, your gifted discernment and tenacious faith in the sacredness of this work guided us through all of the ups and downs of the journey.

Sarah and Alex, the privilege of being your mother has been the greatest joy and honor of my life. Thank you for always believing we could do this work.

How can I thank you, Ander, for thirty-five years of tender love with no expectations, enlarging faith, and joyful moments beyond measure? How many people ever experience this transcendent gift? I love you.

CATHY: My personal and professional life have been profoundly impacted by three mentors who have formed me vocationally and deeply encouraged me spiritually: Drs. Gary Moon, Beth McEntire, and Leo Rotan.

My beloved Crens, my second family. How can I possibly thank you for all you have given me through all of these years?

Kitty, my spiritual friend, and coauthor. My own hidden life would have gone impoverished without your willingness to invite me, all those years ago, into a friendship with you and our dear Betty. I am eternally grateful that I have always been able to count on your guidance, wisdom, forgiveness, and enormous capacity to make everything so much fun. Karen, Betsy, Mary Helen, Bill—pure gifts, four siblings who cheer for and stand with you, come what may.

Mom and Dad, I am grateful for all of your generosity and your loving support of both of us through this process, and mostly for your faithful prayers. I love you.

And to the Beloved, from Whom all blessings flow, for He has given us everything. It has all been sacred gift.

NOTES

1. In reflecting on this entry in my journal some forty years later, I can only say this: God's compassion is not something abstract or distant—it is close and intimate. Jesus came to be with us in our suffering. It is in Christ that we see the fullness of God's compassion. I simply, as best I could, from the depths of my brokenness and pain, placed on paper my response to such compassion.
2. Dietrich Bonhoeffer, *The Cost of Discipleship* (New York: Macmillan, 1963), 103.
3. Dame Julian of Norwich, *The Revelation of Love in Sixteen Showings* (Ligouri, Missouri: Ligouri/Triumph, 1944, 1977), 192.
4. Julian, 106.
5. Julian, 127.

ABOUT

THE AUTHORS

KITTY CRENSHAW, 55, is a homemaker, mother of two grown daughters and the wife of U.S. Congressman Ander Crenshaw (R-Florida). Kitty has served on numerous civic and charitable boards and has been a long-time advocate and fund-raiser for various Christian ministries and community organizations. Kitty and Ander reside in Jacksonville, Florida, and Washington, DC. She speaks from her heart and out of the rare experience of having been mentored by and enjoying a spiritual friendship with Betty for over forty years.

CATHERINE SNAPP, 41, resides in Tallahassee, Florida, and holds a PhD in educational psychology from Baylor University with a research focus on spiritual development and faith formation. She holds a master's degree in counseling from Georgia State University and a diploma in Christian counseling from the Psychological Studies Institute. Cathy is currently in clinical practice, working primarily with depressed populations, on faculty in the Department of Behavioral Medicine at the Family Practice

Residency at Tallahassee Memorial Hospital in Florida. As a clinical practitioner, she is especially qualified to speak to and teach about the psycho-spiritual dimensions of attaining wellness. She has known and been spiritually mentored by Betty for over fifteen years.

Both authors are available to speak at conferences, seminars, workshops, and retreats.

For more information or materials associated with *The Hidden Life*, please visit our website at thehiddenlife.com.

THERE IS GRACE FOUND IN HARDSHIP.

On Broken Legs

Through the wilderness of a shattered spirit, award-winning author and journalist Wendy Murray Zoba learns what it feels like to walk with God on broken legs. This beautifully written literary memoir shows us how God uses personal crises to both shatter and rebuild our faith.
Wendy Murray Zoba   1-57683-643-6

Calm My Anxious Heart

Although many Christian women say they trust God, their lives are filled with worry and anxiety—about their children, finances, relationships, and jobs. They know their lives should be characterized by faith in God, but they're unsure of how to get that kind of faith. This book helps women grow in contentment as they address their barriers and how to overcome them.
Linda Dillow   1-57683-047-0

When I Lay My Isaac Down

For the first time, best-selling author Carol Kent shares the heartbreaking story of her son, Jason, with the world. Her moving testimony to God's faithfulness will alter the way you think about personal challenges.
Carol Kent   1-57683-474-3

Visit your local Christian bookstore,
call NavPress at 1-800-366-7788, or log on to www.navpress.com
to purchase.

To locate a Christian bookstore near you, call 1-800-991-7747.

NAVPRESS
BRINGING TRUTH TO LIFE
www.navpress.com